MEMORIES OF THE
Lincolnshire
Fishing Industry

Bernard Bale

COUNTRYSIDE BOOKS
NEWBURY BERKSHIRE

First published 2010
© Bernard Bale 2010

COUNTRYSIDE BOOKS
3 Catherine Road
Newbury, Berkshire

To view our complete range of books,
please visit us at
www.countrysidebooks.co.uk

ISBN 978 1 84674 213 2

Designed by Peter Davies, Nautilus Design
Produced through MRM Associates Ltd., Reading
Typeset by Mac Style, Beverley, UK
Printed by Cambridge University Press

Contents

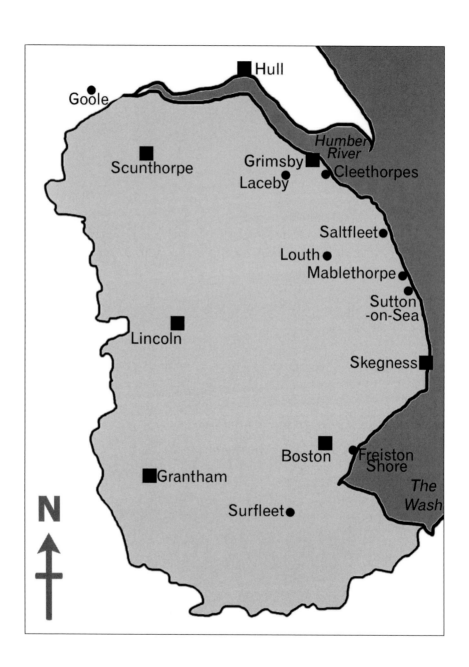

Introduction

For some it is a plate of delicious, golden-battered haddock accompanied by a pile of hot, crispy chips. For others it is a mouth-watering prawn cocktail, artistically presented. It might even be a sophisticated sea bass with saffron sauce. Whatever your seafood preference – Harry Ramsden or Rick Stein – there would be no choice at all if it was not for those special men who brave the elements, sleep little and work hard in life-threatening conditions to bring back to shore the harvest of the ocean.

There are few braver and harder-working than the fishing men of Lincolnshire and, of course, their families, for whom each trip is a sacrifice of shared time with the ultimate price constantly hanging over their heads. If heaven is fish-shaped, these people are angels.

What do you know about the fishing heritage of Lincolnshire? Perhaps you, the reader, are a part of it. If so, then hopefully you will find this book a memory jerker and it will remind you of your own particular experiences, the things you have told others or perhaps kept to yourself for those quiet, private moments. If you know very little then you are in company since I am a writer and broadcaster first and foremost and my knowledge of the fishing industry was even more limited than the exclusion zone around Iceland. That being the case, we shall take the voyage together and discover whatever there is to find.

The book takes us on a cruise into the history and tradition of the Lincolnshire fishing industry from its very beginnings, through to the recent past and even a little into the future.

Some of the tales are nail-biting, some are funny and some just touch the most raw of emotions but they are all a part of this fascinating way of life and its very special people.

Bernard Bale

Chapter 1

Fishing in Lincolnshire – The Early Days

Perhaps **it is hard to imagine** that Grimsby was once the busiest fishing port in the world. If so, then it might be even more difficult to believe that fishing was a thriving industry on the Lincolnshire coast even before the Romans came, saw and conquered the region. It was probably the resident Coritani tribe who set the ball rolling. Although they were primarily a peace-loving, agricultural people, they enjoyed the odd haddock netted from the ocean and were not against trading their catch with anyone who asked.

When the Romans settled in Lincoln and spread their soldiers and workers to other parts of the county, some found a lucrative occupation in panning salt from the sea. The salt was popular since it had preservative qualities which added considerably to the 'eat by' dates of both locally farmed and caught meat and, of course, fish.

Those Roman workers discovered that by catching their own fish as well, they could cut out the middle man.

After a few centuries of Roman settlement, the Danes arrived, liked what they saw and created Grimsby. How it got its name is something of legend since there is an unproven tale that one very special Dane by the name of Grim became honoured with land and celebrity for rescuing and raising orphaned Prince Havelok of Denmark. As the prince grew up, he helped in Grim's fishing and fish sales business. Havelok never forgot his rescue by Grim and when he reclaimed the Danish throne he honoured him and gave him enough money to create a new town – Grimsbye. There are a lot of Lincolnshire towns and villages ending with –by, which simply means settlement. Examples include Saltfleetby, Somersby, Utterby and Spilsby.

There was still no fishing industry as such although, clearly, it was well on the way both in the Grimsby area and further down the coast where the population was spreading into double and triple figures. The pastures were green, the trees were plentiful and the fish visited the coastline at least twice a day. All this was, of course, a while before stretched and stressed King Harold lost his ultimate home match against the Normans at Hastings in 1066. One of the earlier projects of the Norman regime was the Domesday Book of 1086 and we find Grimsby with its name in that famous ledger, marked as quite important for both its fishing and its trading port. Grimsby thrived along with other areas of the Lincolnshire coast and its fishing reputation spread.

In 1201 King John decided it would be a good idea to award a Royal Charter to Grimsby in recognition of its contribution to British life. John had the unenviable task of raising money, mostly through taxes, and he had to keep the economy on an even keel to fund the vast amounts his brother Richard (the Lion Heart) had spent on fighting overseas. Grimsby was not only feeding the nation but also its economic success meant that its business owners could make a larger than average contribution to the Treasury. That was very pleasing to King John, of course, and hence the Royal Charter. Obviously, the king was also delighted with its contribution to his personal table and, doubtless, its contribution to the Royal tax collection. Grimsby was now well and truly on the map with a population of nearly 2,000.

Of course, where there is money there is self-interest and subsequent controversy. The growing Grimsby fishing industry was not immune to such carryings-on. Even as the Royal Charter was on its way there was a row as fishermen from Filey landed their catches at Grimsby. It appears that the local Abbot of Wellow had awarded himself a percentage of everything landed in his patch and the God-fearing fishing folk of Grimsby did not wish to incur the wrath of the Almighty so they went along with it. However, there was a similar arrangement in place across the Humber where the prior of Bridlington held claim over a portion of fish landed by its locals. The Filey fishing fraternity doubtless found it a strain to give a cut to their local branch of the Almighty's network and did not take too kindly to the Abbot of Wellow also having his finger in the fish pie, so to speak. The matter was eventually resolved, although it did resurface on more than one occasion. How the Almighty must have held his head in his hands as he witnessed the mercenary antics of his ground crew.

It might seem that Grimsby never looked back after gaining its Royal Charter but in fact it has hit more than one decline over the years, including during the 15th century when locals sought financial help from London, claiming that the area was now virtual wasteland. The problem had been with the River Haven silting up so badly that shipping traffic almost came to a standstill, with a serious demise of the fishing trade.

Grimsby bounced back of course, thanks to some positive thinking and the re-siting of port entrances but by the end of the 16th century its population was decimated once again when the plague struck, Whether it came from inland or from the ships docking in its busy port is still debatable but it struck hard and turned Grimsby temporarily into a ghost town. The spirit of those fishing folk would not be killed off though and the town survived yet again.

During this time records of fishing activity and who owned what were taking shape and we are grateful today to be able to search those primitive archives to be able to get a clearer picture of the fishing fraternity and their agricultural links. It also indicates that these fishing folk did not stay within sight of the shoreline but were adventurous and quite prepared to take on the might of the North Sea well away from home.

In 1424 Richard Burton from the Clee area is recorded as having gone on a fishing voyage to Iceland, quite an undertaking in those days. How well he fared has not been entered into the written annals of history but clearly if he had not returned safely that would have been worthy of mention.

We can also discover more about the fishing industry during these centuries by looking at some of the wills of deceased land and boat owners. In 1532 John Mason of Itterby left the bulk of his estate to his wife and son. That estate included shares in both cogs and boats. Cogs were a small craft peculiar to the Humber area while the boats were somewhat bigger and carried an actual crew. One of Mr Mason's interests was in a five-man boat, which was considered to be quite large at the time.

Two decades later Richard Beatniffe left a couple of herring nets to Henry Oldham and a mare and two ewes to one Bartholomew Preston who also had the benefit of receiving a mare, a pack-saddle and various bits and pieces in the will of his father, Thomas Preston. From all of this, we glean that herring fishing was quite predominant and also the link between farming and fishing, as well as something which does not at first seem very relevant. Thomas Preston's occupation is listed as fishmonger and it seems that the mare and saddle pack was his delivery van all those years ago in the 16th century.

In June 1582 Thomas and Brian West both died, quite possibly in an accident at sea. Neither man had made a will and their estates were valued by a team of appraisers. Among the goods they left were two cogs owned by Brian West and valued at £4, as well as some shares in other boats. Thomas West's goods of value were listed as nets and lines worth then about £1 2s (£1.10) and some pieces of string. Presumably the latter was tied up in his estate. This information reveals that through those centuries the fishing industry in the area was as tempestuous as the sea upon which it depended. Values of goods changed fairly frequently during those early decades and centuries which reveal that the fishing industry was subject to serious decline followed by restoration.

Just as the actual fishing business changed, changed and changed again so did the demand for various fish and other creatures of the sea. Oysters, for instance, became more and more popular and were quite plentiful in days gone by. In the early 18th century they were particularly in demand and the fishing folk were happy to oblige. Any assessment of wealth was certainly looked upon in hand-rubbing manner if oyster equipment or indeed oysters themselves were part of a man's belongings.

As fishing reached the Victorian era, it had had more ups and downs than a rowing boat crossing the Bay of Biscay. But each time, it survived and strengthened again – and not just in Grimsby. Further down the coast there was a parallel in Boston, famous for its role in sending some of the Puritans on their way to America in the wake of the Pilgrim Fathers who had made the journey a decade earlier. Boston had both a thriving port and a fishing business, which have survived feast and famine to this day. While some of the Boston boats went into deep waters, others found a good living in The Wash which is still popular today, especially for shellfish collecting.

Other coastal towns also developed their own fishing interests alongside their constantly expanding agricultural activities. Interestingly, Sutton on Sea is now a demure mini-resort which caters as much for those seeking a peaceful retirement as those holidaying away from the beer and chips of neighbouring Mablethorpe. Sutton, though, could easily have been a major player in the fishing industry. In the early 19th century Sutton was chosen to become a fishing town because of plans to create a fish dock. The North Sea Fisheries, Harbour and Dock Company was founded to make and run the proposed fish dock, which was to take some of the pressure off Grimsby and Hull which were booming at that time. It had been decided that Sutton was to be included on a new railway line so it seemed that the town was headed for unexpected wealth and popularity.

The railway did make its way to Sutton (and stayed until Dr Beeching decided otherwise in the 1960s). Land prices in the area soared and Sutton was about to enter a financial dreamland until the whole project collapsed in 1907, mostly because those attempting to serve their own best interests could not agree the best way forward.

Ever heard of Freiston Shore? Possibly not, but you definitely would have if you had been around in the early 19th century because it was almost a Blackpool of its time – without the illuminations, piers, tower and arcades, of course. The sandy beaches were glorious and attracted visitors from as far away as the Midlands. There were fairs and race meetings on the beach, and hotels which were always busy. It was possibly this popularity which persuaded the fishing folk to capitalise on the many visitors rather than develop their own industry, for fishing had been an occupation there for many years. Even during the tourism boom of the 1820s there were a number of fishing boats based at Freiston Shore and they kept up a steady supply of miscellaneous fish, as well as shrimps and the ever-popular oysters. Tourism was an easier option so fishing became more of a local tradition than a business investment.

We jump ahead though, for there is more to reveal about the development of fishing in Grimsby in the 18th century. Grimsby then was looked down upon simply because it was considered to be an outpost, a victim of its geographical location. In some ways that has not changed but certainly while the industrial revolution was sweeping the country, Grimsby maintained its role as a fishing port, untouched by what was considered to be the trendy progress of the day. Perhaps that was a good thing but it certainly meant that the town was cast even more adrift by the powers who arranged transport and postal services. The village of Grimsby was not worthy of a full timetable of stagecoach services since nobody wanted to go there anyway. Why would they? It was just a little fishing place with little fishing people and a bit of a port. It was probably on its last legs anyway. Those who thought that way looked only at the surface. They failed to see the grit and resolve of those fishing families who were to play such an important part in keeping Grimsby afloat, even though it was touch and go at times.

During the 18th century the fishing industry of Grimsby went through a bad patch. It is difficult to fully understand because the business had actually expanded and moved on a great deal from the simple concept of going out in boats to bring in fish. Oysters had been farmed for some time but now they were being bought as far away as Scotland and transported to Grimsby for processing and selling. More allied businesses, supplying equipment, had also sprung up but, whether there were not enough real businessmen to balance the books or whether there was a lack of real investment into other business opportunities, it is not easy to decide several centuries later. The fact is that the people were generally very poor, the population waned to below a thousand and the area nearly imploded. Thank goodness that the grit we previously mentioned ensured that there was no ultimate collapse. In fact, some investment finally came into Grimsby in the form of a group of well-off country residents who decided that they could make even more money by redeveloping the port, which had become stagnant through the notorious silt.

As the Grimsby Haven Company, they both succeeded and failed. They did get the port working again but encouraging more business seemed to be beyond them. They tried all sorts of things to bring in the money, even whaling which was being carried out successfully elsewhere. They just could not tap into the market, however, and the Promised Land for Grimsby never really came into view. It was a failure yet it was also a success, since it kept the place alive and optimistic long enough for the railways to reach the town and open a very large door to prosperity.

It was John Chapman, chairman of the Manchester, Sheffield and Lincolnshire Railway, who had the foresight to get the railway extended to Grimsby. He saw that there was great potential in the town despite its lowly status and, along with insisting on the railway extension, he also made sure his company acquired the rights to the Grimsby Haven Company, thus enabling a new dock to be built. When John Chapman retired from his role as chairman of the company he was replaced by another dynamo of commerce and enterprise, Edward Watkin.

Sir Edward, as he became, was a hard man. He would not listen to any opposition and steam-rollered his way through life to get what he wanted. He was not a modest man and often claimed to be the sole reason Grimsby not only survived but prospered. He was probably right. He was honoured with a knighthood and a baronetcy and there is no doubt that he had a tremendous influence on the turnaround in Grimsby's fortunes, but he was not a popular man. Nobody dared to so much as whisper a word of dissent in his presence, or even in the presence of his lackeys. He made sure people in high places danced to his tune or lost their lofty positions. He even placed local politicians in power at the expense of democracy. Whatever his motivations, Grimsby certainly felt the benefit and in half a century under the rule of these two very different men, the village in decline became a town in ascendancy.

This was an incredible era for Grimsby. The new Royal Dock was not really created with fishing in mind but John Chapman realised that fishing could not be overlooked. The more he examined the industry the more he was convinced that Grimsby could become a major player again, perhaps *the* major player. He didn't miss a trick in encouraging local fishing folk to get out into the North Sea where the fishing stocks were abundant and to bring their catches home to Grimsby to sell and then get straight back out to sea. When he heard of a dispute between Hull fishermen and their docks, John Chapman offered them a much

An aerial view of the modern docks at Grimsby. Times and facilities change but the legendary dock tower continues to preside over life in the town.

better deal to bring their fish to Grimsby. The Hull men duly started to land their fish at Grimsby and John Chapman and his fellow directors created a new fishing company and funded a brand new dock, custom-built to meet the requirements of the fishing industry. By the 1850s more than 500 tons of fish were being landed regularly each week at Grimsby and the railway now proved invaluable as it transported that fish inland for consumption. Profits were starting to roll in for everyone involved and with some reinvestment the business increased amazingly. A decade later, the new dock was operating at full tilt and that 500 tons of fish had increased to an amazing 10,000 tons.

By the 1880s more than 800 fishing smacks were now operating from Grimsby and the accompanying trade in ropes, nets, supplies and other necessary equipment was booming. Oh yes, not forgetting the benefits afforded the sail makers, for up to now you had either rowed or sailed your boat. Life was good for those people but it was soon to change once again. The steam revolution was about to happen.

As the 19th century entered its last decade, the steam engine found its way into specially-designed trawlers. Of course there were those who said it would never catch on but many took a more optimistic view and quickly embraced the new technology. So, by 1892, there were 113 steam trawlers and 799 smacks. Within another decade it had changed again. The smacks were gone and Grimsby had 450 steam trawlers based at its vast dock.

During its peak, this was the fishing fleet of Grimsby. You could walk on water from trawler to trawler. These vessels were all in dock at the same time because of an industrial dispute, an occasional event in the history of fishing.

Not everyone was happy about this. There were those who wanted to cling to family tradition and found it hard to cope with these new developments. Steam had brought about so many changes both inland with the spread of the railways and, now, at sea where the concept of time and the rugged lifestyle was altered for good. Some fishing folk gave up their work altogether and embarked on new careers as shopkeepers or rail workers. But as some left their fishing roots behind, other innovative roots were being established with new fish merchants and allied businesses.

Take a walk through the docks today and see the many varied businesses collected together to serve the industry. It was no different then. Every trawler and its crew needed food supplies, weather-proof clothing, drink and tobacco, tools, ropes, nets, fuel and so on. Every

Yes, that really is a pile of fish all salted and ready to go on sale.

fish merchant needed transport, wooden boxes, stationery, bank accounts, rat catchers and so on.

One thing didn't change and remains today as an iconic landmark which welcomes those fishermen of yesterday and, of course, today's fishermen with their modern approach to fishing. Yes, you are right, we are talking about the famous Grimsby Dock Tower. The Tower is here to stay since it is a Grade I listed building and you cannot get much more protection than that. The reason for such status is that it was built in 1851 and acclaimed as the tallest brick-built construction in Britain at 309 ft high. It has a 350-step, cast-iron spiral staircase and a wrought-iron tank holding 30,000 gallons of water, which reveals the point for its construction. It was created to provide the necessary water pressure to operate the gates of the then proposed Royal Dock. In other words, it is a giant cistern but a quite remarkable one. Fishermen of the last 160 years have keenly squinted from the ocean to catch a glimpse of this wonderful landmark which stands today as a tribute to those who have served the industry, both those whose hands have become calloused at sea and those whose investments put the town on the map in such a major way.

By the start of the First World War, Grimsby had emerged from its centuries of life in the doldrums, with an occasional glimpse of economic sunshine, to become a much-celebrated and bustling town where the work remained hard but the pubs were busy and the families could say with pride that they were from Grimsby. It had been an exciting revolution for Grimsby which was now arguably the busiest fishing port in the world.

Elsewhere in the county there was also progress. Boston played its part in the steam revolution and, like Grimsby, the population grew and with it the facilities in the area. The port was booming and so was the fishing industry in that part of the world. Catches were larger and more efficiently landed than ever before and fishing smacks became a thing of the past, kept more for nostalgia than practicality.

Lumpers busy at work in the docks. Speed is of the essence. The barrels have long since been replaced by heavy-duty plastic boxes – or kits as they are still known.

Lincolnshire as a whole, from the coastal hamlets like Saltfleet to the inland city of Lincoln, felt the benefit of the fishing boom. On the coast they were fishing while inland they were transporting for or supplying the industry. The three natural industries of Britain were fishing, farming and mining and Lincolnshire had two of those in abundance. There is no doubt that by the start of the 20th century the county had become one of the most important and wealthiest in the land.

The First World War years saw progress put on ice but after 1918 and even though the world's economy was in a mess – not for the first or last time – Grimsby continued to blossom. The trawlers brought back larger and larger catches and produced greater and greater profits for all. A trawler skipper had a new-found status as a result of his wealth, and being the wife of a trawler captain meant that you were either very high in or even top of the pecking order in your social circle. It was not just the skippers, though. Everyone involved had a share in the boom, whether an ordinary trawlerman or a major fish merchant. Walk along Freeman Street now and it is in serious need of investment and an overhaul but in those heady days of the early

20th century it was a thriving thoroughfare where much of the fish was sold and where trawlermen and their comrades of the land-based sales and fish processing businesses let their hair down. The pubs were always full and the entertainment places always well patronised.

Grimsby was able to celebrate its status as the world's most successful fishing port, supplying a fifth of all the fish consumed in Britain, and that status continued past the Second World War and into the 1960s, even to the 1970s, when the boom in frozen foods brought even more investment to the town. It seemed that Grimsby could do no wrong. After centuries of striving, Grimsby and other coastal towns of Lincolnshire were enjoying a life that they had richly earned through sheer determination and hard work.

So, where did it all go wrong – or did times simply change along with fashions and trends? It definitely went wrong. The initiative and enterprise of the past seemed to desert the present when a major upset started the decline of the fishing industry in Grimsby. Whereas the pioneers of the past were prepared to roll up their sleeves and make necessary changes or demands to protect their interests, the generation of the 1970s appeared to have forgotten or lost that spirit of the sea and simply sat back and moaned as their industry was taken apart by one major incident. It is summed up in one word – Iceland.

Indeed, the Cod Wars of the 1970s (see chapter 3) made a huge difference to British fishing and the greater the local economy relied on that industry, the harder it was hit. It was probably the closest Britain and Iceland had ever come to actually going to war. In the event the long-winded negotiations finally reached a settlement, signed in Oslo on 1st June 1976. It was agreed that a maximum of 24 British trawlers would be allowed inside the 200-mile exclusion zone at any one time. Icelandic politicians returned home as heroes. British politicians returned home feeling that they had saved face. The fishing industry though, in particular in Aberdeen, Hull and Grimsby, was devastated. The massive deep sea fishing fleet of Grimsby, with its distinctive GY registration, was decimated very quickly as both men and boats idled in the dock area. The fishing port went from bustling to brooding, almost in mourning for the loss of its major activity.

All was not abandoned though. A little deep sea fishing remained, while some of the more enterprising turned to shallow-water fishing. With their usual work diminished, the fish processing factories adapted to take on additional projects such as frozen pizza production.

In recent years Grimsby has maintained its association with fishing despite the struggle of the industry and the seeming indifference of politicians. It has relaunched itself as a food town with all kinds of processing and cold storage available. The fishing boats can still be seen in dock or to-ing and fro-ing. A trip to the docks with all its allied businesses is as fascinating as ever, even though it is almost a ghost town by comparison with its teeming past. Make no mistake though, Grimsby and its fishing is far from dead. In recent times history has been repeated as fishing boats from other ports have been encouraged to land their catches in Grimsby and even bring their processed fish to the town for storage or distribution.

In Boston there are still a healthy working number of boats bringing in small fish, crabs, lobsters and a vast range of other shellfish. In addition there are fishing merchants and allied traders keeping Boston's fishing interests very much alive. The small landing port provides a brief step back in time but there are plans to create a state-of-the art new landing port for the fishermen, a sign of confidence in the fishing future.

Elsewhere along the coast there are still small businesses involved in fishing and what has often thought to have become extinct is, in fact, still living and breathing. Farming, fishing and mining meet the basic requirements of this island race. All three have been devastated in recent decades but they have never actually been finished forever. Neither has Grimsby nor its fishing cousins along the Lincolnshire coast. They may appear to have drowned but they still keep their heads above water and, who knows, perhaps that high tide of success of the past may once again return to refloat the fishing economy.

Chapter 2

Fishing at War

Britannia may rule the waves but it has been a pretty close thing a few times and the Royal Navy has had to dig deep and call on extra help now and then. A valued and famous part of that help has come from the fishing industry, with trawlers being turned into combat and reconnaissance boats and trawlermen into a gritty and determined element of the war machine. Lincolnshire's fishing men and women have played their full part in those activities which have kept the enemy at bay.

The use of fishing boats for military purposes did not start with the Second World War. It did not really begin with the First World War either since the fishing folk from around this great island were often the first to give the alert of would-be invaders. Throughout history there have been incidents of keen-eyed fishermen enabling attacks to be thwarted simply by eliminating the element of surprise.

Let us start though with the First World War, a time when Grimsby was certainly a busy fishing port. A tenth of the local population answered Lord Kitchener's call and joined up as infantrymen, around 8,000 in total. That figure was swollen considerably when the fishing men also went to war. Grimsby alone supplied 433 trawlers and nearly

6,000 men to the war effort while others continued to risk their lives in bringing back fish while running the gauntlet of the extra hazards supplied by the enemy. The country needed both military and food and Lincolnshire answered the call magnificently and at great cost since 156 trawlers were sunk or taken captive. Nearly 1,000 lives were lost, leaving almost as many widows and even more orphans. Grimsby and the rest of the county were scarred forever. The war memorials testify to the ultimate price paid for what was supposed to have been the ultimate victory.

The very first trawler victim of the conflict is said to have been the *Tubal Cain*, which was destroyed by enemy gunfire on Thursday, 17th August 1914. Interestingly, 'Tubal Cain' is allegedly a Masonic password, not really surprisingly given to a trawler since the Freemasons have had such an influence on the Grimsby fishing industry for very many years.

Another of the first victims of that First World War was the *Fittonia*, a Grimsby trawler which proudly carried the identifying number GY390. The *Fittonia* had been on a trawling trip in the North Sea and was on the way home when eyewitnesses on the distant *Barratoria*, a Hartlepool-based commercial steamer, saw an explosion. Seven men went down with the *Fittonia* but there were two survivors, who did not know exactly what had caused the explosion but generally considered it to have been a mine. The two men, deckhand Olsen and trimmer Barnard, were placed in the care of the Shipwrecked Mariners' Society. The date was 2nd September 1914 and the *Fittonia* was surely one of the very earliest victims of the conflict.

There is also the amazing story of the *King Stephen,* or GY1174. During the latter half of the First World War she was commissioned by the Admiralty to serve as a decoy ship but that was by no means the start of her war career, since she had been embroiled in a controversial wartime incident a little earlier.

It was on 2nd February 1916 that the *King Stephen* was fishing in the North Sea in reasonable conditions, although there was heavy cloud in the early hours of the day. Skipper William Martin suddenly saw a light and a shape in the dark which were like nothing he had seen before. He put his crew on alert and had the nets pulled in, just in time for it to become clear that what they could see was the wreckage of a German Zeppelin. They had come face to face with the enemy in unexpected circumstances.

Now a great dilemma presented itself to the captain. There were survivors shouting to be picked up from their place on the wreckage but there was a large group of them, more than his crew, and they were also armed. They would have no difficulty in taking over his trawler if they were so inclined. He struggled with a decision. His mate, George Denny, later recalled: 'It was a decision none of us wanted to make but the skipper had to do something. In the event he put the safety of his men and the boat first and turned away from the scene. The Germans were furious of course and called us everything but the skipper had made up his mind even though he had nightmares about it for the rest of his life.'

In fact, that incident hit the headlines all over the world. In Germany, skipper William Martin was public enemy No 1 while here in Britain he was something of a hero for taking such a tough decision. Despite the support from press and public, the skipper never did get over it and died less than a year later still with the anguish nagging at him.

The *King Stephen* lived on though and became a Q-ship, a decoy which still looked a simple, peaceful trawler but was actually packed with arms and was equipped with carrier pigeons to send intelligence messages back from its meanderings in the ocean. However, there was another sad twist in the tale of the *King Stephen*. Her name had become famous and not been forgotten by the Germans so when she came face-to-face with the enemy again in the form of a German High Seas Fleet, she was instantly recognised. Yes, that's right, the British 'intelligence' at the time had disguised the unfortunate trawler but forgot to change her name and identification. She was sunk and the crew taken prisoner. When they reached the shore they were given a hard time, first of all stoned by an angry German mob and then beaten up before being incarcerated for the rest of the war. Despite that unhappy ending, the *King Stephen* and all who sailed in her were the epitome of bravery and added something special to the legend of trawlers at war.

The *Leo* was another trawler which came to an unhappy end after years of service to the industry and the country. The *Leo* was one of the earliest steam trawlers, having been built in 1904 at Cochrane's Shipyard in Selby for the Grimsby and North Sea Steam Fishing Company. She was requisitioned by the Admiralty in 1917 as part of their Fishing Reserve. When the First World War was over she returned to civvy street and in 1921 was bought by Edwin Bacon.

Leo's service to fishing was interrupted again in November 1939 when once more she was requisitioned as an auxiliary patrol boat during the Second World War. Again she served faithfully, until 29th December 1942 when she set out from Grimsby for the last time. She was lost with all hands.

The surviving trawlers and trawlermen of the First World War eagerly returned to their first-chosen occupation after decommissioning in 1918, but two decades later they were called back to service. Like the *Leo*, some of the same boats and men found themselves once again in the front line. Among them was Joseph Winney, chief engineer of the *Rutlandshire*, who was believed lost when the requisitioned trawler was sunk off Norway. Then, after some time of sadness, Mr Winney was discovered alive and well, along with other crew members, including another Grimsby man, Albert Barker of Barcroft Street.

Once Joseph Winney was reunited with his wife in Tennyson Street, Cleethorpes, his tale was revealed. The *Rutlandshire* had been attacked by up to 20 German planes. The crew of 27 put up a fight while trying to run for cover but the vessel was damaged beyond help and eventually they took to the lifeboats and managed to scramble ashore on the

Norwegian coast, with only one of them suffering a bullet wound. They found an empty house in which to hide and were eventually contacted by people from a nearby village who took them to safety, fed and clothed them and after a few days helped them with transport back to Britain.

'All I can say is that the Norwegian people were simply wonderful,' said Albert Baker. 'They really took care of us and helped our safe return.' Joseph Winney too paid tribute to the Norwegians and his skipper, a Naval officer: 'He also took total charge of the situation and never stinted taking care of us as individuals.'

Perhaps the greatest tribute was to the *Rutlandshire* herself. 'She was a fine vessel and seemed to put up a fight all of her own,' said Chief Engineer Winney. 'Even when she was clearly going to sink, she did her best to get us as near as possible to shore before she finally lurched forward and sank. She was a brilliant example of the skill put into making a British trawler.'

Trawlers were put to all kinds of uses during the two world wars but one particularly dangerous task was minesweeping. Rear Admiral H.G. Thursfield went on record during the Second World War and explained: 'Minesweeping, of course, comes almost naturally to the fishermen who man the trawlers. The task of handling and towing the minesweepers is almost the same thing as their ordinary occupation of handling the trawl.' He added that it went without saying that the trawlermen knew all about bravery by the very nature of their civilian work and were a valuable asset to the war effort. No wonder that Grimsby was the largest centre for minesweepers during the Second World War.

Other trawlers were requisitioned as anti-submarine craft. They might not have had the armoury of the specialised naval vessels but they could pack a punch nevertheless. The U-boats they faced were vulnerable to attack while on the surface and a kitted-out trawler with a 12-pounder gun could prove to be quite an adversary. They did not have the fire-power to force a U-boat to dive but could make life uncomfortable enough to help a U-boat skipper decide that it might

HMT Northern Pride, *seen here on patrol in her role as an anti-submarine vessel in the Second World War. (An original painting by Steve Farrow)*

be a better option, even though underwater the U-boats were slower and vulnerable to depth charges. The trawlers carried a good stock of depth charges as large and powerful as many of their custom-built comrade vessels so there was a good chance that they could cause some serious trouble or even destroy a prowling U-boat.

There was another bonus in using trawlers – they and their crews knew all about rough seas and, while some destroyers and other naval ships might run for shelter, the ocean-wise trawlers would keep going. Whaling ships were also requisitioned, accustomed as they were to working in all conditions, but the trawlers were used for all the major work and many a supply vessel delivered its cargo safely, thanks to the gritty determination of the keen trawler escort boats.

Grimsby trawlers were not confined to the seas of their native coastline, they travelled far and wide. Two of them, the *Staunton* and the *Drummer*, were sent to Brightlingsea in Essex and thus began a sad but incredible final chapter in their story. The *Staunton* was originally built for the Standard Steam Fishing Company of Grimsby in 1907 but was requisitioned in November 1914 and became an auxiliary patrol vessel, changing from GY350 to FY710. She successfully negotiated her way through the First World War and returned to her original job as a trawler in 1920. Just 20 years later she was requisitioned once more in June 1940, again as an auxiliary patrol vessel.

She had been in service for only a month and on 26th July was out on night patrol during a thunderstorm, when enemy bombers roared across the sky. There were no survivors to tell exactly what had happened but it was generally considered that the *Staunton* hit a mine and sank. There was also a report of something falling from the sky, which makes it possible that the *Staunton* was bombed. Skipper Wilfred Campbell and his crew of 17 perished; all but one of them was married with children and most were from Grimsby. Deckhand Joseph Robinson of King Edward Street, Grimsby, left a wife and six-year-old son, almost repeating history since his own father had been lost at sea when Joseph was just two years old.

The *Drummer*, GY1097, was a little younger than the *Staunton*, having been built in 1915 and gone into service as a minesweeper. She was named *Dragoon* for her military work but renamed *Drummer* in 1919 when she was sold to Consolidated Fisheries of Grimsby. After 20 years of faithfully trawling she found herself back in military service in 1939, once again as a minesweeper. Like the *Staunton* she was also sent to patrol the waters around Essex, based at Brightlingsea.

On 4th August 1940 she set out on patrol at around 6.30 pm and a few hours later a huge blast was heard back at Brightlingsea. The *Drummer* was the victim of a magnetic mine. Other vessels in the area managed to rescue most of the crew but four men were killed. The incident took place very near the location of the sunken *Staunton*. Thus, the two Grimsby trawlers were destroyed within nine days of each other and sank to their watery graves less than 400 yards apart. They were not sister ships but have been related in history ever since.

HMT Northern Gem, *(sister ship to the* Northern Pride*), seen here in action during a contact with a U-boat. (An original painting by Steve Farrow)*

In some ways the Second World War came at a fortuitous time for the fishing fleets of Grimsby and also Hull. The industry was suffering a little because of supply exceeding demand and a number of trawlers had been taken out of service. In Hull many of them had been sold off but the boat owners of Grimsby took a wiser move and simply mothballed their vessels for a while. Thus it was that they cashed in quite handsomely when the Admiralty came shopping. Some reports suggest that more than £2 million changed hands for vessels, but that was largely kept from the public since there were so many Grimsby families dependent upon the fishing industry and the thought that trawler owners were simply selling off their livelihoods would not have been well received by the hands.

There was a disgruntled mood in the town but that was largely quashed when it was announced by the Admiralty that they would be recruiting hands to take the requisitioned vessels out to sea. By the time it was also announced that the refitting work would be carried out by Doigs in both the Grimsby dock and the Humber Graving Dock in Immingham, leading to more employment, the spirit of optimism had returned to North Lincolnshire. Grimsby MP Sir Walter Womersley and Louth MP Colonel Heneage had joined forces to put the case for the county doing the refitting work and both became local heroes as a result of their success.

When the war began to get serious, Grimsby's fighting spirit came to the fore and any feelings of displeasure at the way boat owners were handling things were swiftly swept aside. Grimsby itself, along with other towns in the county, was soon under attack. The Germans were not only seeking to demoralise the populace by bombing large towns but also to cripple areas which might be beneficial to the Allies' war effort, as well as striking at the heart of the Royal Air Force which had a major presence in Lincolnshire. Grimsby, Scunthorpe, Boston, Louth, Lincoln, Grantham and just about everywhere else in the county came under attack.

Not all trawlers and men went to sea to fight. Some simply continued fishing and in some ways that was an even more daunting prospect than escorting or minesweeping. The trawlers that went out to sea to bring home food were unarmed and many without radio contact.

The *Grimsby Evening Telegraph* of the day reported on the exploits of several of these unarmed fishing trawlers which were attacked in the early months of the Second World War when the Germans were intent on demoralizing through destruction. These fishing trawlers survived against remarkable odds.

The *Orpheus*, GY35, was one such trawler which, on one occasion, was 100 miles out on the North Sea and about to commence fishing. Two enemy bombers caught sight of her and zoomed in for a closer look. The captain, George Dartnell, told his crew of about eight men to take cover while he alone went to the bridge and took the wheel. He had no means of fighting and had to rely either on zig-zagging the boat or on the planes leaving them alone.

The planes did not leave them alone. They swept in very low over the boat and opened up with machine-gun fire. On their next pass over the helpless trawler the first plane machine-gunned and the second dropped bombs, four in all. Three missed, but one just hit the starboard and damaged the hull sufficiently to cause a major leak. The planes then flew off. All this time the skipper had been spinning the wheel first one way and then the other to make the trawler a less easy target. He never flinched even while under fire and then managed to safely return the *Orpheus* to Grimsby, where his crew celebrated their survival and the remarkable, selfless leadership of their captain.

Another trawler, the *Rigoletto* was about 85 miles from Grimsby when she was attacked by an enemy aircraft which peppered the trawler with machine-gun fire and then bombs. The captain, again, took total control and sent his eight-man crew below decks, except for the mate who was at the winch to put the hose into operation as incendiary bombs began to drop. The captain came under further machine-gun attack while he was in the wheelhouse and, sadly, he was hit and killed. When the mate was also killed, the *Rigoletto* was in big trouble. The third hand, Thomas McArthur, took over and even rushed from the wheelhouse to pick up a blazing incendiary bomb and hurl it overboard. The plane made one further attempt at bombing and strafing and then flew away, leaving the trawler with two dead, damage to its deck and engine room and with several small fires. The rest of the crew turned to and, with the help of a large swell on the ocean, managed to put out the fires. The third hand led by example and they successfully returned to Grimsby, more grateful than ever before to step back on dry land and ready to sing the praises of Thomas McArthur, who was decorated for his action.

The *Eroican*, GY74, was about 70 miles out from Grimsby when she was spotted by an enemy aircraft and immediately came under attack. Skipper Herbert Osborne sent his crew below and remained on the bridge. The plane attacked with machine-gun fire and a shower of incendiary bombs, which set fire to various parts of the trawler. Between attacks the crew dashed out and threw the incendiary bombs overboard while pouring water on the burning areas of the boat. The captain continued to zig-zag the vessel to make it difficult for the attacking pilot. After one last attack the pilot flew away, satisfied that he had caused sufficient damage. He obviously underestimated the resilience of Herbert Osborne and his crew, who safely returned the *Eroican* to Grimsby.

James Sadler was skipper of the *Lavinia* and he was decorated for his bravery and action during an attack on his trawler. He and his crew were about 85 miles out of Grimsby on a heavy sea with icy weather which made the deck treacherously slippery. It was mid-morning when an enemy aircraft came calling. The skipper and his mate were on the bridge and as soon as they heard the hum of an aircraft they sent the crew to the galley for cover. The plane wasted no time in dropping half a dozen bombs, damaging the deck. One bomb was an incendiary device and burst into flames. The skipper immediately rushed out, picked it up and tossed it into the ocean. The pilot wanted to finish the job and rained more bombs in several waves of attack. The skipper stood his ground and kept throwing the trawler from side to side to confuse the pilot. It is believed that 40 bombs were dropped by the plane before it finally flew away. There was some damage to the boat but nobody was killed or wounded other than for a few burns and bruises. Lesser men would have immediately set off for home but James Sadler and his men continued their work for another week before arriving back at Grimsby with a full load of fish and a tale to tell.

These are just a few of the many stories involving Grimsby trawlers during the Second World War. At the start of that war there were 381 vessels fishing out of Grimsby but that figure dropped to 66 in December 1942 before rising again. To put that into perspective, at its lowest point in the Second World War, Hull went down to just one trawler still fishing.

Grimsby Fishing Heritage Centre's resident guide, John Vincent, a former trawlerman from a dynasty of fishing folk, summed up what war meant to the fishing industry in Lincolnshire: 'We all know that every part of the country was changed by both world wars. Lincolnshire was no exception. It is worth remembering that fishing families from Boston and elsewhere along the coast all played their part in defending the country but Grimsby was the busiest fishing port in the land at the time and was certain to be the most involved in the wars.

'It began with families wondering about their future because the industry was going through a strange patch with more fish than we needed being landed. That meant that prices were low and owners were running at a loss. It was a worrying time both at the start of the First World War and the Second World War. It is strange how history repeats itself.

Then when we went to war for the second time in 1939 the worry changed. Work was no longer a problem but rations and staying alive became the focal points. Still, there is usually something good to come out of distress and the people of the area rallied to the call. The men showed great courage and strength in putting to sea to face the enemy, while their wives, girlfriends and children and in many cases, their parents, also showed a strength of character in supporting their men. If anyone ever feared the worst but hoped for the best it was those people during that awful time. They were perpetually steeled for bad news. They were the same during peacetime because it is a tough and dangerous job going out to sea on fishing boats and trawlers, but when people are trying to kill you at the same time, it is even tougher.

'Churchill paid tribute to trawlermen and their families at the end of the last war and he was right, the British fishing industry and, for me, especially the Grimsby area, was owed for its work and sacrifice in keeping this country free.'

There are a number of war memorials in the Grimsby area in honour of the men that died during the two world wars. One such token is the memorial island at the Queens Steps, Lock Head, Grimsby Royal Dock which was created by RNPS veterans and can be viewed by obtaining a day pass at the Royal Docks office. It commemorates the men of the Royal Naval Patrol Service, or 'Harry Tate's Navy' as it has become affectionately known. Harry Tate was himself held in great affection as a comedian and impressionist who made a huge name for himself both on stage and later on screen before his death in 1940. Harry Tate's Navy typified the English characteristic of not taking itself too seriously.

By way of my own tribute, these are the Grimsby-stationed trawlers that were sunk or destroyed during the Second World War:

Agate	*Gael*	*Proficient*
Akranes	*Gloaming*	*Red Gauntlet*
Bahram	*Harvest Gleaner*	*Remillo*
Benvolio	*Henriette*	*Sea King*
Calverton	*Loch Alsh*	*Silicia*
Cap D'Antifer	*Lord Selborne*	*Solomon*
Cape Spartil	*Lormont*	*St. Cyrus*
Cloughton Wyke	*Luda Lady*	*St. Donats*
Corfield	*M.A. West*	*Strathborve*
Cortina	*Mann Prince*	*Susarion*
Dervish	*Meror*	*Thora*
Fairplay	*Othello*	*Valdora*
Faraday	*Princess Victoria*	*William Stephen*

More than 4,000 Grimsby lives were lost at sea during the two world wars. As the inscription on the memorial says:

THEY GAVE THEIR ALL SO OTHERS COULD BE
FREE WE WILL REMEMBER THEM

Chapter 3

War in Peace

The fishing industry performed over and above the call of duty during both world wars and thousands of lives were sacrificed on the altar of conflict. Relief came when peace was declared and technically we have been at peace ever since although we all know that we have actually been at war at times. Amongst the conflicts was that of the so-called Cod War.

Far from being a modern act of aggression, 'Cod Wars' go back to at least the 19th century when Iceland and one or two others objected to other nations – and the British in particular – fishing in what they claimed to be their waters. As an example, in early 1899 a steam trawler called *Sargon* was fishing in the Faroes when the weather turned bad and the skipper had to seek shelter in Fubleford harbour. A Danish gunboat arrived, ordered him to pay anchorage and then told him he must leave.

There were many such incidents at that time, with around 23 Grimsby and Hull trawlers being 'arrested' and fined. One particularly hostile situation arose in April 1899 when the *Caspian*, a steam trawler under the command of Captain Charles Henry Johnson, was approached in the Faroes by a Danish gunboat claiming that the vessel was inside the then 25-mile limit. The skipper refused to stop and the gunboat fired a few rounds of blank shells before raising the stakes by using live ammunition. Eventually, after some dangerous manoeuvres which almost caused a collision, the trawler was forced to stop.

The situation did not get any better as the captain was ordered aboard the Danish vessel. He quickly told his brother, Bill, to make a dash for it. The gunboat, with the skipper on board, was taken by surprise and could not catch the escaping trawler. Shots were fired but the *Caspian* managed to get away and eventually arrived back in Grimsby with bullet holes to prove the story.

Meanwhile on board the gunboat, the *Caspian*'s skipper remonstrated with his captors who thought he was going to hit their captain. As a result, he was tied to the mast until they returned to shore where he was in court the next day and sentenced to 30 days in custody. The court mostly consisted of the captain and senior officers from the gunboat. Still, it was no easy passage since he was fed bread and water and finally released a much thinner and unwell version of his former self. Protests from Britain fell on deaf ears.

Another skipper, aboard the *Cephas*, was refused permission to prove that his vessel was quite legally fishing outside the 25-mile exclusion zone off the Faroes. He was eventually fined 200 krone and had some equipment and fish confiscated

All that – and more – was going on even before the outbreak of the First World War when Britain was supposedly at peace with most of the rest of the world. At home, questions were being asked by the press, the public and some politicians but diplomats continued a slow dialogue, possibly in the hope that it would all eventually go away. Of course, we know now that it didn't. Once agreement was reached with one country, another started to shake a spear or two.

One of those countries was Russia, or the USSR which was then, in the 1920s, still in its relative infancy. The Russians began to get very fidgety about British trawlers working in what they considered to be part of their territory in the Arctic Circle and sent gunboats to harass anyone fishing there. That is why the British Naval cruiser HMS *Godetia* was despatched to keep an eye on events.

When skipper Jack Waite took his vessel, *Jeria*, from Grimsby to the area in April 1928 he had no idea that he and his crew were about to come under the spotlight of international attention. The captain was not without experience of conflict since during the First World War he had encountered at first hand what can happen at sea when the boat on which he served as mate was destroyed by a German submarine.

It was late afternoon on 28th April when a USSR gunboat appeared and was clearly ready for action. The *Jeria* had become separated from the other trawlers in the area and was an easy target for the Russians, or so they thought. The skipper decided to make a run for it and ignored the sirens and signals from the gunboat. It was snowing and getting dark but that did not deter the gunboat from its pursuit.

Things were looking rather ugly so Captain Jack fired a distress flare in the hope of attracting a British Naval vessel. A responding flare told him that he had been successful and it was not long before HMS *Godetia* was on the scene. The commanding officer told the trawler skipper to get on his way and leave the gunboat to the Royal Navy. The Russians took one look at the much bigger and commanding British military ship and sped away into the darkness.

Agreement was later reached on fishing rights but in general there has always been an uncomfortable feel about close encounters between British trawlers and their Russian counterparts or, indeed, their minders who show the flag now and then. One such occasion was in September 1938 when the *York City*, under the captaincy of Henry Ford, was stopped and told to go, along with two other British vessels, the *Dalmatia* and the *St Attalas*, to Kildin Island. Skipper Ford tried to make a run for it but his vessel came under fire three times so he decided to go along with the order. Soviet officers came aboard and searched the ship, allegedly looking for cameras and guns – note the order of priority. Finding nothing of any importance, the officers then accused the skipper of fishing within a no-go area. He refuted it and after some deliberation he was told that he would be free to leave the following day. It was a storm in a tea cup but this was one beverage the Grimsby men found hard to swallow and it certainly left a nasty taste.

Perhaps the most famous fishing arguments, however, have been between Britain and Iceland. Although agreements had been reached between the two countries in the late 19th century, a growing uneasiness broke into open hostility in the latter months of 1958 when Iceland suddenly passed a law that extended its fishing rights.

Between early September and mid-November tensions ran high as fishing trawlers from Grimsby carried on business as usual under the protective eye of four British warships, who did have to intervene from time to time. HMS *Russell* was kept fairly busy as Icelandic gunboats became more and more threatening. She was forced to deliver several ultimatums and even collided with one patrol boat to prove a point.

Eventually settlement between the two countries was made and everybody relaxed for a while. One of the points of the agreement was that if any future conflict occurred it would be put before the International Court of Justice in The Hague for arbitration. The Cod War was over – or was it?

No, it wasn't! On 1st September 1972, Iceland did it again. This time they extended their fishing rights to 50 miles off their coastline. Just to put the record straight, this was a different Icelandic government, a leftist-socialist coalition which arrogantly ignored agreements made by previous governments and was not at all interested in the point about going to arbitration at The Hague.

The arrogance was followed by aggression and no sooner had the new law been passed than Icelandic gunboats were out on the sea chasing off trawlers that were within the 50-mile limit. Some of them were totally unaware of any such new development and at a loss to know why they were being treated in such a manner.

One new development in this action was that the Icelandic force had net cutters and did not hesitate to use them against British trawlers. The British government responded by sending a number of small Naval tugs as protection for the trawlers but general opinion was that this was not enough of a response and only encouraged the Icelanders.

As tension increased the British government started to take the whole matter more seriously, sending in bigger warships. That encouraged people to consider sitting round the table and finally, with the help of NATO, agreement was reached once again. British vessels were to be allowed within the new 50-mile zone but with catch limitations. Everybody relaxed and the seas became calm again – metaphorically speaking.

One of the trawlers that fell victim to the Icelandic patrol vessels was the *Spurs*, in March 1973. Captain Bill Hardie Junior said at the time: 'We were harassed by both the ICV's *Aegir* and *Odinn*. The *Aegir* managed to cut our warps as we were on our last haul of the trip. She was that close to us I could have shaken hands with their skipper. It's a wonder we didn't collide. It was a nuisance but we were just about heading for home anyway.'

It was not just out at sea that Grimsby fishermen ran into hostility. The *Notts Forest* put into Thorshavn, on the Faroes, for repairs but the work stopped halfway through because local union members who sympathised with the Icelandic stance, simply downed tools. Not to be beaten, the *Notts Forest* was patched up well enough to take her custom elsewhere.

The *Aldershot* seemed to be under attack every time she went anywhere remotely near Iceland. On one trip she found herself in direct conflict with the ICV *Aegir* which had singled her out for attention from a number of other trawlers, some of which manoeuvred to make the passage of the Icelandic gunboat difficult. *Aldershot* skipper Eddie Collins told the patrol boat officers that he did not recognise the new limit and was not prepared to stop fishing. The *Aegir* was then aimed at the trawler, cut her warps and collided with her stern, causing a lengthy gash which then started to seep water. The crew kept patching the hole with everything from planks to mattresses as Skipper Collins headed for Torshavn.

That was not the end of the controversy as some demonstrators kept untying her mooring rope and made it impossible for the *Aldershot* to dock for repairs. She went instead to Skaale where her repairs were carried out successfully.

'We later received a letter of apology from the Faroese, which was nice', said the skipper. 'We were victimised every time we went back on a fishing trip though and I started to wonder what exactly the Icelanders had against us. They seemed to pick on us more than anyone else.'

He was right it seems, since the *Aldershot* had been in quite an encounter in 1964 when the then captain Leslie Cumby was in charge. There was another 'arrest' of the *Aldershot* in 1965, with a lengthy court case in Iceland and another back in Grimsby. The skipper and his crew were exonerated. Mr Don Lister of Consolidated Fisheries Ltd claimed that the *Aldershot* was being victimised by the Icelandic ICVs and said 'It seems to me that this ship is being victimised. It's always the *Aldershot* that's attacked.'

When hands were shaken to signal the end of the second Cod War everyone hoped that this time the hostilities were really at an end. The peoples of Britain and Iceland had previously had a good relationship with many incidents of co-operation and life-saving by and for both sides.

Peace was not to remain for long though and in November 1975 Iceland extended her exclusion zone yet again, this time to an incredible 200 miles. The hostility began instantly and the British government publicly refused to recognise the new exclusion zone. Once again, trawlers found themselves in a tense situation as Icelandic gunboats cut their nets and even rammed them. The Royal Navy was sent to protect the British trawlers and they did not flinch.

Their presence was valid but the British trawlers did find themselves on the receiving end of some great harassment and were shot at with live rounds on many occasions. In the end Iceland's claim to 200 miles exclusion was largely adhered to but with a number of less painful clauses to be finalised in what was actually an informal agreement.

There has been little trouble since then but even when we are in a state of peace, there is no doubt that most skippers are keeping an eye open for another flare-up. Those foreign aggressors forgot an important point. They failed to recall that Grimsby is in Lincolnshire, the county where the people will never flinch from a physical attack and where determination is such that no problem cannot be overcome.

Chapter 4

Fishing Families

Fishing is such a hard and hazardous business that it makes you wonder why anyone would want to take it up as a career. Perhaps it is the challenge, or a love of the sea, or simply the desire to do something that is not a 9 to 5 office job, but there are those who do willingly apply to join the trawlers – and for some it is the start of a dynasty.

The fishing industry is full of dynasties, yet of course they all funnel back to a time when someone decided to go to sea for the first time and hoped they would return to tell the tale with some cash in their back pocket. For others there was no choice – they were pressed. It would be unfair to say that the Grimsby apprentice system was basically another name for enforced work for orphans but in many cases that was true. During the 19th century someone had the bright idea of recruiting boys from workhouses and reformatories and thus a little over half the new deckhands were from those backgrounds.

Some went on to make a career out of it and even become wealthy boat owners, but sadly there were many others who perished or were seriously injured, mostly because they were inexperienced and given jobs to do which were beyond their capabilities. As you will gather from that, the boys were not held in high esteem and many were badly treated to say the least. Bullying was rife, especially in cases involving recruits from reformatories. The boys may have been sent there in the first place for only a minor offence but were sometimes treated as if they were hardened criminals and had to be put down before they caused trouble. Many reports of brutality came back to shore and more than one or two murders.

There have been very many cases of men disappearing overboard. In many of these incidents the 'accidental death' verdict is totally accurate but close-lipped fishermen have often hinted at whether the missing crew member jumped, fell or was pushed into icy waters. There is, however, inescapable evidence of violence on board such as was recorded on Saturday June 3rd, 1967 when Aberdeen Sheriff's Court heard a Grimsby fisherman plead guilty to a charge of assaulting deckhand John Campbell with a gutting knife on the *Blackburn Rovers* as the vessel was steaming to the Icelandic fishing grounds. The skipper had to put into Aberdeen where an ambulance and the police met the vessel. James Ode was sent to prison for six months for the assault.

In July 2nd, 1971 the *Gillingham* was leaving the dock when a member of the crew by the name of Hewson suddenly jumped ashore. Shortly afterwards, Hewson was seen by John Macdonald back on board and covered in blood. Another crew member, Graham Horsfall, said Hewson had fallen down the ladder. The cook, Derek Smith, picked the man up but was told by Horsfall to leave him there. Later on, Macdonald went to the galley and Horsfall, accompanied by another man, Jim Padgett, followed him in. Horsfall then began to attack Macdonald, knocking him to the ground where the attack continued, causing severe bruising to his back, body and arms, the back of his head and several cuts to his face. Eventually, Macdonald managed to escape and go to the wireless room. Later on, the cook, Derek Smith, went to his berth. Horsfall and Padgett followed him in and Padgett began to punch and kick him. Smith managed to escape the attack and get to the bridge where he collapsed. Smith had to have several stitches to a cut above his right eye. Both his eyes were black and swollen and he had a suspected fractured nose, a swollen face and cut and abrasions. Because of the trouble on board, the *Gillingham* returned to Grimsby.

Other apprentices who put to sea were treated differently, especially if they were the latest offspring of a known fishing paterfamilias. One such was John Vincent: 'I was eight when my father first took me on a trip,' he recalled. 'It is a fishing family tradition that boys go out for a maiden trip at around that age. You are old enough to take in what is happening but there is little you can do to help. It is a kind of baptism thing with everything going on around you.

'It was a great experience though and by the time I came back I knew where my future was going to be. I don't know what it was that was the greatest appeal. Perhaps it was a successful voyage, bringing home food for the nation and a pay packet for the family, maybe it was simply being out on the sea which is a world of its own, the camaraderie on board or just the fact that I wanted to be like my Dad. I don't know. I just knew that I was hooked from the start and I have never regretted it.'

As for the families themselves, there have been many famous names associated with Lincolnshire fishing; famous that is if you are involved in the industry. If we go back in time to the mid-16th century we come across the name Stables, or Stapylls as it was written on his probate inventory. William Stables owned half a cog boat, a small inshore fishing vessel. Upon his death that half share in the boat was worth about 5s 7d (or 27p). His total fishing equipment was valued at 14s (70p). The will might not be worth contesting now but it was a

Cod fishermen in the earlier part of the last century rarely had time to pose for photographs but these gentlemen could not resist it – until the skipper caught them. Then it was back to work!

considerable asset then and there have certainly been other men by the name of Stables who have taken to the sea to bring fish ashore. Whether they were related or not is difficult to establish but the idea of some of today's trawlermen on their modern vessels being related to William Stables of five centuries ago is, at the very least, a good yarn.

And here is a good old Lincolnshire name – Manby. Thomas Manby lived in Cleethorpes during the late 17th and early 18th centuries and when his will was published on 5th January 1728 he left two boats and a quantity of oysters, among other things. His fishing interests amounted to £6, not as much as his farming interests but still a tidy sum in those days and he was certainly not the last Manby to be involved in fishing.

Another name that crops up regularly in Lincolnshire is West and many trawlermen have rejoiced in that surname. Brian West was around during the reign of Queen Elizabeth I and fishing was his chief occupation. He owned a small boat and had a share in another, as well as enough equipment to run a full fishing business. His brother, Thomas was more of a farming man but he also had fishing interests and it seems that they were together when they died since they both passed away on the same day in June 1582. A fishing accident is the suggested cause of death. When he died, Brian's will allowed for a distribution of his goods among quite a few people, including other close relatives and thus the fishing tradition continued. There are still members of the West family going to sea today.

Mention the name Osborne and everyone knows who you are talking about since they are a local family who did well in the fishing trade and formed A & R Osborne. Many Osbornes have served on trawlers both during peacetime and wartime and there were those who perished while serving their country. Look through the lists on the many memorials to trawlermen lost and the name Osborne will appear quite a few times. You will also see the name Bannister, which is readily associated with Alfred Bannister Trawlers Ltd. Alfred began life in 1868, born into a poor railway family but started his working career as a cook on a fishing smack. His optimistic approach to life and sheer hard work later led to him owning a fleet of trawlers which just grew and grew. He never lost track of his roots though and was a much loved and respected member of the Lincolnshire community and a great ambassador for the area's fishing industry. His success was tinged with sadness due to the loss of his son Raymond who enlisted with the 1st Battalion Lincolnshire Regiment in the First World War and was killed in action. The rest of the family went into various careers but the Bannister trawler business continued and as a tribute to the man who started it all, Alfred Bannister Mews can be found in Laceby to the west of Grimsby.

Is your name Taylor? Then you may be interested in William Henry Taylor who became famous in the fishing world despite his very humble beginnings. William was not a local lad but heard that there might be work in the industry in Grimsby so he walked, yes walked, all the way from Bristol. Once again it is a tale of endeavour since Harry – as he became known to his friends – worked his way from the lowest to the highest, owning a fleet of trawlers under the banner H.L.Taylor Ltd. The business flourished through the 20th century until finally calling a halt to activities in 1981. The name Taylor is still revered in Lincolnshire and national trawler circles.

There are many tales of those who were either born locally or found their way to the county and especially to Grimsby in the hope of finding fame and fortune – or at least a regular meal on the table. It seems that the fishing industry certainly turned the area into a land of opportunity. Arthur Jeffs was born into a very large family from Ramsgate in 1866. Work and career opportunities were not abundant so he and his brother, Charles, found their way to Grimsby, worked on trawlers and before long had their own business which not only blossomed into a large fleet of vessels but also expanded into an engineering business with particular service to fishing. The engineering firm even outlived the trawler business, which eventually went the way of so many others.

Names like Nickerson, Butt, Ross, Robinson, Bacon and many others, too numerous to mention, have all earned their place in the history of Lincolnshire fishing. They have that common thread in that they have created something very special, showing the same gritty determination that has seen the entire industry survive rough economic seas, as well as the real oceans from which they have earned their fame and indeed their fortunes.

There were opportunities for those with ambition and the desire to work hard. Peter Fenty of Cleethorpes went to sea for the first time in early 1950. Six years later he became the youngest skipper in Grimsby at the age of 21 as he took charge of the *Vanessa Ann* and took her out on what was to be a successful maiden voyage as captain.

Then, of course, there were those who did not have the ambition or the desire for responsibility other than providing for their families and watching out for their fellow crewmen, as John Vincent of Grimsby's National Fishing Heritage Centre explained: 'For many men they were happy enough to have work, get paid, spend some time with their families, go to the pub and then go back to sea. It was a simple although hard life for quite a few of them. They did not really want to own a trawler and many of them did not even want to be a skipper even though it meant a much better income. They just didn't want responsibility. It is much the same today. Not everyone going to sea on a trawler has his eye on taking over the job but that does not mean that he is not of absolute value. Those men are diamonds because they will give you an honest day's work for an honest day's pay and you can't want for more than that when you are out on a trawler.'

While the men were away it was left to their wives to be head of the household, to make sure the money lasted until next pay day, to feed and clothe the children and to be ready for when their husbands returned to shore.

'It was a hard life for them,' said John. 'It still is in some ways but not the same as it was. Families were usually larger in years gone by, homes were smaller and did not have the mod cons of today. There was not the money available and there were certainly not the benefits. You couldn't cook in a microwave or send out for a pizza like you can now. There is no doubt that in many ways it was harder on the families than it was for the men themselves. For some of the young women, getting married to a fishing man was a culture shock. It was all right if they came from a fishing family themselves because they knew what to expect but if they didn't it was like entering a different way of life totally.'

Trawlermen led a very hard life on board and would be away for days and sometimes weeks on end. They had certain expectations when they returned and that is one of the reasons why they usually

Repairing nets was always a tedious task. Of course, it was an essential job though most of those who did it regularly developed hands like thick leather gloves.

fathered a larger-than-average family. Quite often babies were born and did not meet their dads for some weeks. Family life was often split into two different phases. When Dad was home, family life would usually centre around him. When he was away it was different and the children had to learn to cope. Many of them also had to learn that Dad had three homes – his boat, his cottage and the pub.

Drinking has long been a part of the seagoing culture and certainly the fishing industry is no different. Young wives will tell you that even before they were married they were sometimes shocked to see their intended slumped on the pavement outside their house after turning up to take them out. They often had to usher them away before their parents saw the state of them. Those girls all thought they would be able to change the love of their life. Most of them were wrong, of course.

They either learned to live with it or gave up and went home to Mum – or into the arms of someone more understanding. The trouble with drinking was that it cost money and time, and sometimes turned a benign character into an aggressive and moody person to avoid. Fights outside – and sometimes inside – the pubs were common and some wives had a ready-made excuse for the black eye they would be sporting for a few days when hubby was home.

That is generalising, of course, and it would be unfair to pin that kind of label on every man that ever worked within the Lincolnshire fishing industry but it was nevertheless an unfortunate trait. 'Many were good husbands and fathers, of course,' said John Neville. 'A lot did care for their families and hated being away from them but they

---

Maybe the men were out there risking their lives on the ocean but the women did their bit too and worked hard for pretty low wages to help the fish on the way to the table. Notice that they are working outdoors – nice in the summer but …

knew it went with the job and if you wanted work in difficult times you just had to keep at it. Fishing families often stuck together and supported each other and that probably made the whole fraternity even more close, which was just as well as women left to fend for themselves with four or five children would have found it almost impossible without help.'

The fishing families almost created their own village within the community. Some still do. Most of them know each other and will come together socially if possible. The social events organised by skippers' wives used to have some notoriety in the area. Evenings at the Winter Gardens in Cleethorpes were often riotous affairs as the ladies let their hair down. The fishing folk who lived together also laughed together, sang together, drank together, often shared what they had and were there for each other as much as their personal circumstances allowed. They also shared something else, especially the women. They shared fear.

How often we have seen images of miners' wives standing at the colliery gate waiting for news when there was a problem underground. The wives and mothers of trawlermen know what it is like to feel like that and perhaps even worse, since they sometimes do not even know where their husbands and sons are. When a boat is late and then reported missing they anxiously await news of a rescue, a sighting or even sometimes just news of wreckage that will at least put them out of their misery. Some will stand at the dock gate with their unblinking eyes scanning the horizon for sight of something, anything. Others will busy themselves with anything, shelling peas, washing up for the umpteenth time, anything that will distract them from the dread of bad news, the potential tears, the gut-wrenching moment of telling the children. When a trawler goes missing the whole community is hit hard. Differences are forgotten in the common cause of hope. Cups of tea are poured by the gallon and if people didn't smoke before they are tempted to take it up to ease their understandable tension.

In days gone by when communication was not as easy as today, wives and mothers kept a constant vigil either at the dock or gathered in front of the radio waiting for news. They did their best to keep the worry from their children but their tears were never far away and those children usually knew that there was a problem and that dad was in danger. Sometimes the bad news came quickly, while at other times it might be weeks before the search was called off or a piece of driftwood was found and the full story of what had happened emerged. When the worst was realised, the whole community went into mourning – as now. Men that had perhaps not been the most popular were mourned as much as anyone else, their sins forgiven and forgotten. They were among the seafaring comrades who had fallen and were remembered with equality of sincerity and love. One part of the community was hurt and the whole of the community was in pain.

Of course, it was not always bad news and there have been many tales of dramatic rescues, fishing boats that have limped home under the cool expertise of a brave skipper and his courageous crew. Then the tears are different and the smiles are only interrupted by the kisses of relief and welcome home. The whole fishing family celebrates the safe return of its sons who will recover at home before risking their lives again as they depart on another voyage to bring home food for the nation. That is the chosen lot of the fishing family, a unique breed with a unique lifestyle.

Technology has changed and brought many new skills and gadgets to the industry but the ocean remains as it has always been, sometimes benign, sometimes volatile but always dangerous.

It takes a special breed of people to meet it head on and to wait at home for the safe return of their loved ones.

Chapter 5

The Times, They Are A-Changing

I t is hard to imagine life before the motor car and the same can be said of a fishing industry which has all the benefits of satellite information, computerised technology, modern communications and many other labour-saving devices. If the fishing folk of centuries past could just take a glimpse at today's larger and modern 21st-century vessels they would be totally amazed. In fact they probably would not believe their own eyes. Yet the basic principles of the work remain much the same and the ultimate ambition remains exactly the same as they have done since someone first set out with a small net and a rowing boat.

In an ongoing quest for more for less, fishing folk – like everyone else – have steadily evolved their industry. Ideas were taken and adapted from other industries and also from other fishing ports and villages around the country, and overseas, of course. The Dutch, for instance, introduced an early trawl in the 17th century but the Brits turned it into the kind of trawler which became the prototype for so many others. It became known as a *dogger* – a Dutch word for a simple boat operating a trawl net. English fishermen quickly saw the advantages, improved it and put it into operation. The trawler was born and the fishing folk of Lincolnshire were quick to adopt it as it was perfect for harvesting the North Sea. Needless to say, the Dogger Bank we hear about on shipping forecasts owes its name to being a favoured fishing ground of dogger skippers.

Brixham in Devon takes the credit for major changes in the 19th century when local people designed a vessel that could take the trawl into deeper waters. The red sails of the new boats inspired the famous song *Red Sails in the Sunset*, but fishing fleets all over the world saw the potential and copied the new vessel design. Lincolnshire was no exception and there were soon new areas of deeper sea fishing being explored and harvested.

In a sense it revolutionised fishing since there were now much greater options for the industry. Most boats at this stage were owned by their skippers but, of course, as time went on, that was to change when the true financial possibilities of fishing became obvious. Investors were prepared to back changes but expected to profit by them so the need for good financial returns was critical to the industry. Changes also included different styles of vessels. In addition to trawlers there were drifters and these along with some of the bigger trawlers were helped out to the ocean by special paddle tugs which provided some extra power to the usual sail.

Another revolution came about in 1881 when Grimsby and Hull led the way in converting from sail to steam simultaneously. The two ports were in such competition that they both acted swiftly to keep up with each other. Specialised vessels were being introduced at frequent intervals to meet the differing needs of deep sea, shallow waters, shellfish, differing fish stocks and so on but the move to steam was to change the face of fishing forever, although there were still vessels operating by sail up to the First World War. Coal-fired steam engines made a huge difference to efficiency and speed in reaching fishing grounds and when the diesel engine took over during the latter part of the 20th century, the vessels of the fishing fleets turned into high-powered ocean-going trucks.

Changes in fishing were not restricted to how boats were powered, of course. Even the fish that were sought changed. For instance, herring fishing only really began in 1819 when a plentiful supply was found in the Moray Firth. As trawling developed it became possible for more boats to tap into this new source and herring fishing became not only popular but big business. Certainly Grimsby fishing folk brought home many a fine catch of herring along with the more regular catch of cod.

Other fish demanded further innovation. For example, the beam trawler was designed primarily for catching flatfish, the trawl system created to get to the very depths where those fish spend most of their time. Other vessels have been designed especially for harvesting crabs, lobsters, crayfish and others. Still more have been adapted to bring home shrimps and molluscs. Every element of fishing has been revolutionised to ensure that it has its own specialist vessels to make the job as efficient and productive as possible. The good fishing folk of Lincolnshire have never been slow to embrace change and have often been at the cutting edge of experimentation, no mean feat when sometimes those trials can mean the difference between returning home and being lost at sea. Trawlers have often been hired specifically for the scientific research which ultimately draws conclusions on fish movements and population, as well as other environmental and ecological issues.

The technological advances on board have also had an impact on the lives of fishing crews. Imagine the value of experience in the fishing industry a century or more ago. Skippers and their crew members were expected to be capable seamen who knew all about splicing ropes, natural navigation and what to do in an emergency.

They also needed to know where the best fishing grounds were for which fish and how to get there, fish safely and successfully and return home in good time. They also had to be capable of very hard physical work, surviving on little sleep, with food that was rarely of good quality and often in atrocious weather conditions. There are still strong elements of that today of course but there is little doubt that given the choice fishing folk would prefer the life aboard modern trawlers.

What has changed? Navigation, for one. Fishermen of old gazed at the stars to help them plot their course. Today they are more likely to gaze at the onboard sat-nav. Autopilot is used on board many vessels today, including trawlers and even smaller fishing boats. An autopilot is a mechanical, electrical or hydraulic system which basically takes over the guidance of a vessel without the need for human intervention, It is much the same as the autopilot used in aircraft and is not only useful for following a course but also in keeping correct distances when fishing in pairs or amid a group of trawlers.

Radar and sonar both play their part in fishing. Radar often links with the autopilot while sonar is more than useful in sounding out water depths, as well as locating shoals of fish. A couple of hundred years ago these possibilities would almost have been considered to be witchcraft!

Even relatively simple modernisations such as winches have made such a difference. At one time nets were hauled aboard by simple manpower, with muscles bulging and hardened hands ignoring the rope burns. Then came winches which made the job that little bit easier and more recently came power winches, which in turn have taken away some of the regular back-breaking chores. Modern trawlers make full use of all this technological advancement, especially since most of it can be controlled at the press of a button on the bridge – or wheelhouse as some prefer to call it. The skipper can settle into the comfort of his chair and press the right buttons at the right time just as he might use the remote control for the television at home. He still has to concentrate though and understand what he is seeing on the screens in front of. The days of yelling at the crew might have long gone but the skipper still has to stay wide awake for very long hours.

Times have changed in the galley too. The cook is probably the most important crew member on board and even he has been provided with labour-saving devices that give him many advantages over his predecessors. Quick-mix sauces, ready-prepared foods, tea bags and microwaves have made it a much easier job, although some say that the end product is not much different to that presented to the crews of long ago. Better leave that debate to those on board!

Years ago, fishing from Grimsby, Boston or any of the smaller coastal villages meant that boats did not go too far and would return, hopefully laden, for quick sales and a return for their efforts. As distances drew longer and catches grew larger there was a need to accommodate greater quantities of fish and to keep them fresh for

Fish sorting, gutting and trimming was sometimes done on board as soon as the nets were emptied which is why these men are knee-deep in fish.

hours or days more than in the past. Packing fish into boxes with plenty of ice was one answer but the need for something a little more sophisticated presented itself and having chill rooms on board was the obvious next step.

Some larger trawlers have become virtual factory ships. Not only have the chilling facilities improved, with in some cases fish being actually frozen into blocks, but now in some cases the processing starts while still at sea, with automatic gutting and filleting machinery employed instead of the many hands that once waited at the quayside to go to work in the vast fish processing sheds.

It could be argued that the passing of the skill of gutting and filleting over to machinery is a sad move and indeed it must be said that the number of men and women working in that role during the heyday of Lincolnshire fishing ran into thousands. The huge sheds were alive with activity from very early in the morning when the fish were landed until the very last processed fish was flung into the very last box which was then taken by horse-drawn cart to the railway station to be sent all over the country to high street fishmongers, hotels, restaurants and other businesses. The atmosphere in those processing sheds was second to none, a sight to behold. They were noisy as men and women sang, joked, argued, laughed and shouted. The atmosphere was pungent and by the very nature of the work at hand it was also very cold and very dangerous, as the sharp knives flashed to quickly do their work and send the fish onto the next link in the chain from ocean to shop.

In 1937 an orthopaedic surgeon by the name of Mr Guy Pulvertaft moved to Grimsby and was to become famous in medical circles for his work there. He was even awarded the CBE. Why? Because he became an expert in hand injuries and hand surgery as a result of dealing with around 30,000 injuries during his ten years at Grimsby, the vast majority of those injuries stemming from the processing sheds of the local fishing industry. The gutting knife was – and still is in

Life in the fish preparation shed was tough. It was quite hazardous as knives were prone to slipping and digits were thus prone to be sliced off. If this was your regular job, everyone in town knew where you worked – no matter how many times you washed!

some places – an essential tool for the job but it has claimed many innocent victims over the years. There is no truth, however, that the idea of fish fingers was spawned in the gutting and filleting shed!

I mentioned the carts drawn by horses which took boxes of fish to the nearest railway station and it was quite a sight at the docks to see perhaps 50 or more horses patiently waiting in harness ready to taxi the fish boxes. Usually the horses were given feed troughs to keep them happy as they waited.

The freezer trawlers are distinctively different from the 'wet fish' trawlers which keep their fish in the hold in wet conditions and often sprinkled with ice. The legislation is also different, with wet fish trawlers having a much more restricted time at sea for obvious reasons. What was once the simple job of going out to sea and bringing back a catch of fish has become quite complex. 'It is a very different way of life now,' said John Vincent. 'It used to be really hard work and hazardous but fairly simple in its actual day-to-day running. Now there is so much technology and red tape that you have to be really clued-up to survive. Many older ones talk about the good old days and they were good old days in many respects but you cannot stand in the way of progress, even if it hurts at times.'

Let us not forget also that there have been other forms of fishing and ocean harvesting through the years and they too have seen many changes. For example, Cleethorpes had large quantities of oyster beds providing a fairly lucrative income for some, even if the oysters were selling at around £1 for a thousand during the mid-19th century. By their very nature oyster beds stretched no more than a mile out to sea from the coastline of Cleethorpes, but still they covered about 300 acres. When the tide was low the oysters could be seen in their thousands and this was quite a magnet for visitors who were politely reminded that this was someone else's property and therefore not available for the taking. 'Pick your own' oysters was definitely out. In fact the oyster beds were tenanted from the then Lord Yarborough.

Something in the region of six million oysters were harvested annually but times forced changes even here on the inshore sea bed. Blame it on the growing population of booming Grimsby and the immediate area or perhaps on the growing number of flush toilets but an increase of sewage flowing into the ocean resulted in the demise of the oyster beds. A couple of cases of food poisoning pointed towards contaminated oysters and the industry collapsed around the early 1900s.

Further down the coast at Freiston Shore, the changing times also put paid to the cottage fishing industry of shrimps, soles, sprats and other inshore fish. What was a steady business suffered after neighbouring Skegness and Mablethorpe were reached by the railway. While they prospered less money was being spent by visitors to Freiston Shore and a mini-recession led to the closure of just about everything in the village, including the demise of the small fishing population who simply could not survive alone.

Boston has managed to carry on despite appearing to be on its last legs as far as fishing is concerned and reflects the story of fishing in

Freiston Shore, now popular with bird watchers, was once a hive of activity for the fishing community. (Courtesy of www.visitlincolnshire.com)

the north of the county. The deep sea trawling that once successfully operated from Boston has given way to a much greater emphasis on cockle harvesting from The Wash. Small boats regularly go out in convoy to bring home a variety of shellfish and other small species, once again taking advantage of the modern technology that has made life just a little easier.

Surfleet is even further down the coast and into the heart of The Wash. It also rejoices in a great fishing tradition and has gone through the same changes, fortunes and misfortunes as the rest of the Lincolnshire fishing industry. Fish and shellfish were once busily landed at Surfleet and immediately sent to Billingsgate Market in London. Today the catches are fewer and the fishing is mostly for sport but who knows, one day the times that are a-changing could herald the return of major fishing to this and other areas along the Lincolnshire coast.

Fishing boats tied up at Boston, soon to head off for The Wash, following in the wake of those who have fished before them down the centuries. (Courtesy of Boston Borough Council and Peter Norton)

Chapter 6

What Is It Really Like?

For those of us whose seafaring experience goes little beyond a ferry to France or Holland or perhaps a trip round the bay while on holiday, there can be little notion of what it is really like aboard a trawler, let alone of leaving the shoreline behind and risking life and limb on the uncompromising ocean to earn a living. Fortunately we have the experiences of others to give us a little insight and we also have the excellent National Fishing Heritage Centre at Grimsby.

Mark Stopper of Boston first went to sea as a 15-year-old in 1975 and spent more time on the ocean than on the land. Renowned for his work on recording the life and times of the fishing industry he explained to me: 'I was bitten by the bug when I was just a boy and never regretted it. My mother was a hairdresser and my father ran a fruit stall so there was no big influence from either of them but I had an uncle who had a boat and the more I saw of the boats in the harbour at Boston, where I lived, the more I wanted to go to sea.

'I had my chance when I was quite young when I was allowed to go out on one of the boats for a short trip. That was it. I was bitten by the fishing bug and there was nothing else I wanted to do. I decided there and then that the fishing industry was where I wanted to be working.'

Mark applied to join the nautical school at Grimsby and along with a pal, Roy Steadman, he was accepted. 'I dropped out after a while but Roy carried on,' said Mark. 'It wasn't happening quickly enough for me. I realised that I had made a mistake though and went cap in hand to ask if I could go back and finish the course. To my surprise I was allowed to return and I did complete the course which included three weeks at sea aboard the *Lord Jellicoe*.'

At the age of 16 he signed up with Boston Deep Sea Fisheries and began a career that is like no other. 'Once you have been involved in deep sea fishing, there is no other life that satisfies you,' said Mark. 'It is a hard life and no mistake. You spend 18 hours on deck but you are guaranteed six hours below during which time you have to both eat and sleep. You tend to snack rather than have proper meals because you value your sleep time so much. You hardly get a proper wash until you are on the way home and the cabin, which usually takes twelve men, is the best place on the planet when it is time to turn in for a while. You tend not to get undressed but just take off your oilskins and thigh boots and throw them onto the pile on the floor.

'More than once I have found a rat in my bed. They get aboard and stay aboard and when you are in freezing conditions the rats know that the best place to keep warm is in someone's bed. Some of them are huge because they live so well on the boats.

'I know that doesn't paint an attractive picture of life on board but there is something about being on a boat in the open sea that is like nothing else. Each trip is an adventure all of its own. You never know what is going to appear in the nets. We have regularly caught sharks of different sizes and also what we call "Monsters of the Deep", which is the name we give to just about anything we don't recognise. I have seen some very strange fish and they are often put to one side and taken back for scientists to research.

'When you are out there fishing you also see whales and other creatures. I have seen whaling at fairly close quarters and it is not pleasant. I am not saying there is no place for it but it is not something I would want to be involved in. The stench from the factory ships travels for miles and the sight of dead whales roped to the sides of hunting ships is not pleasant.'

Like other industries in the UK, the fishing business has hit many problems and its demise has changed the lives of many of those who have been a part of it. Mark Stopper is no exception. 'Fishing virtually stopped and there were not the jobs or trips available,' he said. 'I could see the writing on the wall so I took lessons and gained an HGV licence. That is what I do today but I am still a fisherman at heart and that is what has led me to write books and be involved in the production of videos about the industry and in particular the role Boston has played through the years.

'There is nothing like being out there on the sea and bringing back a good catch. I would not have swapped my chosen career for any other. Yes, it's hard and sometimes you don't think you are going to survive but it just gets into you and you are prepared to put up with all kinds of stresses, all kinds of injuries, all kinds of hardships and all kinds of disappointments because you are a Lincolnshire fisherman.'

As already mentioned, John Vincent is another expert on the industry. 'The first rule when you go to sea on a trawler is not to fall out with the cook!' John explained.

'He might not be the best cook you have ever experienced – in fact there is a good chance that he will be one of the worst – but you keep on the right side of him. He will keep you going with cups of tea and frequent meals and snacks and you really need those when you are working on a trawler.

You don't often find trawlermen very far from a cup of tea!

'To be fair, the cook does not have an easy job and never has had. He has got to keep food and drink available pretty well 24 hours a day in a fairly cramped galley on rations that he has to make last the trip. He has to keep everyone happy including the skipper. That is probably the most difficult part of the job.

'Some cooks are pretty pleasant and take a lot of trouble while others can be total tyrants and treat complaints with more than scorn, in fact downright contempt. Woe betide anyone who falls foul of a cook like that, which is why I said that you just don't fall out with the cook. They have their own problems of course. Trying to cook a meal while the sea is tossing you from one side of the galley to the other is not easy and burns are quite frequent. Perhaps that's why cooks often seem to be grumpy characters. Nowadays they have modern tin openers and devices like that but the fundamental problem of keeping a crew happy and not scalding yourself or carving your fingers off remains the same.'

The cook also has to keep his galley and his utensils clean. An outbreak of food poisoning on board a fishing vessel would not be a pretty situation. There again, the whole boat must return to harbour in a clean condition or its owners may penalise those on board.

'That is how we spend most of the return journey – cleaning,' John Vincent explained. 'When you are travelling to the fishing grounds you spend your time preparing the equipment for fishing. When you travel back you spend the time making sure that the vessel is as immaculate as you can possibly make it.

'Everything is cleaned until it shines and that means more than just hosing things down. Anything that can be polished is polished. Anything that is varnished is cleaned until it shines. The cook has to make sure that his galley is scrupulously clean and, like the rest of the boat, all the equipment has to be stowed in its proper place. The owners used to personally inspect boats when they returned and would fine a crew if they were not satisfied. You may not get the owners personally taking a look any more but the need to return to harbour with an immaculate vessel still exists and is often a matter of pride.'

But what is it actually like to be out there working on the ocean? 'It is not as hard as it used to be,' said John. 'It is still a tough job though and always will be because you can put as many labour-saving devices in place as you like but you still have to face whatever the weather and the sea decides to throw at you.

'I have often been asked which is the toughest job on board and I have never yet been able to answer that question properly. The skipper has the responsibility and has to know how everything works, as well as being able to take the decisions which could mean the difference between a profitable trip and waste of time or indeed the difference between survival and disaster. He has to know all about legislation and

A lumper unloads a smaller catch. Usually these were teams of men but this chap is working alone hoisting the baskets onto a pontoon.

must be a good man-manager as well as a diplomat. He might have less of the physical labour on board and he might have the best quarters but there are many fishing men who would not swap places with him for all the money in the world.

'We have talked about the cook and his hard work but probably the hardest workers of the lot are the deckhands. Think about a three week trip to the Arctic and you will get some idea of what it is like, if you can imagine working in a freezer room on a slippery floor which pitches and tosses much of the time.

'Times have changed a bit but deckhands used to be under the command of the mate and their work ranged from getting the trawl

It's auction time in the early 20th century. This is quite an intense time for both sellers and buyers, not to mention the auctioneer. For onlookers it is great entertainment – if they can take their eyes off the sheer quantity of fish.

net over the side to hauling it back in again some hours later, gutting the fish and stowing it below with ice. They didn't sleep very much during the voyage and often had to be patched up after cracking a rib or slicing a hand, making do with what passed for first aid until they returned home and could get to hospital.

'It has been known for deckhands to work non-stop in freezing conditions for 48 hours without let-up. That is seriously tough. The life of the deckhand has improved but there is still plenty of physical work and one thing that never changes is the length of time you spend breathing in icy air. It can be totally exhausting and that's where the cook plays his part in keeping everybody going with non-stop mugs of tea and snacks.

'Sleep is grabbed whenever possible and usually for only a few hours at a time which means that you cat-nap rather than sleep and you don't bother getting undressed because you have to be ready to spring into action at a moment's notice. You make sure your boots and weatherproofs are nearby at all times. You don't get much in the way of home comforts but most people have mobile phones now so you don't have to be completely cut off any more.

'The attitudes on board are generally pretty good. Men tend to watch out for each other as a rule. It is a little like people coming together to face adversity. It is rare that you get major fall-outs and to be honest most people on board are willing to get on and get the job done together. There are often a lot of laughs and good-natured banter and there is a sharing of gloom when the news comes through that Grimsby Town has lost another match.

'A lot of the crew know each other and have worked together before so they know what to expect. If you get someone who is not just new to the crew but new to the industry, they will get a bit of good-natured ribbing but they will survive that and it will be their turn next time.'

Let us not forget the maintenance work that must be carried out frequently when the vessel is not at sea. Before 1934 when the new Fish Dock was opened at Grimsby and new slipways were introduced, vessels were taken to the Graving Docks which were part of Fish Dock No 1. It was quite an involved procedure since all the water in the Graving Dock had to be pumped out once the vessel was in place and that took some time. The modern equipment brought that down to about 20 minutes which was much more useful because ship owners did not want their vessels out of commission any longer than was absolutely necessary.

A team of workmen would clean off all the barnacles, algae and anything else that had attached itself below the waterline and as soon as it was dry it would be inspected by a surveyor representing Lloyds Insurance. Once he was happy that all was well and safe, the special

Way back in the 1930s, still in the days of real horse-power, dozens of worthy steeds would patiently wait between the shafts for hours before playing their part in taking the fish on the next part of its journey – to the railway station and local businesses.

anti-fouling paint would be coated onto the cleaned-up area. Of course, if any further work was found to be needed it was dealt with there and then, as it is now. Sometimes we forget the team of men who rolled up their sleeves to keep our fishing vessels as safe and well presented as possible. They are still doing it of course and even if the work is not quite as backbreaking as it used to be, the value of the maintenance job should never be underestimated.

But back to life on the ocean wave and the *Grimsby Telegraph*, as the leading newspaper for most of those of the industry in Lincolnshire, has been covering the delights and the despairs of the fishing industry for decades and is compulsive reading for all those involved.

As an example, in February 2010, former deep-sea fisherman Michael Sparkes of Grimsby, revealed life on the trawler *Stoke City*, one of the many vessels named after football clubs as we shall see later. 'I first sailed on the *Stoke City* in 1962 because my regular ship, the *Churchill*, was being re-fitted' said Michael in his *Grimsby Telegraph* interview. 'I decided to do one or two trips on the *Stoke City* in the meantime.

'We set sail from the North Wall of Grimsby Docks one early December morning when the snow was falling heavily and making conditions very bleak indeed. She was skippered at the time by a man called Ivan Bass, a Canadian who was an experienced Icelandic fisherman.

'His mate was a big chap too and his name was Sid Mears, whose wife ran an off-licence. Nearly all the rest of the crew were older than me as I was just a 17-year-old deckhand at the time.

'I remember the ship being a happy one to sail on. I also remember that, although she was an older ship she turned out to be an excellent sea ship in bad weather, which surprised me at the time. On that trip we went to the North Cape of Iceland and experienced terrible bad weather conditions. We had gales, black frost and icing problems for most of the time and most of us had frost bite on our hands, lips and feet.

'We spent quite a few hours on deck chopping ice off the *Stoke City*'s superstructure to stop it getting top heavy. Thankfully we managed a good catch on that trip, having around 1,600 kits to land back in Grimsby on the market. [A kit is the name given to the baskets in which fish were landed; baskets having since given way to boxes.]

'Sailing home in bad weather our steel bobbins broke loose one morning and the mate sent me and another deckie, Norman, to secure them because they were rolling dangerously about the deck. As we stepped off the ship's casing we saw a tremendous sea coming at us on the starboard side. I managed to duck beneath the ship's rail which meant it went over me with its full force. Poor Norman was washed over the winch by the wave, badly injuring his back. He later spent quite a while in hospital recovering after we arrived home and decided not to do deep water fishing off Iceland any more.

'On the whole we accepted the dangers of life at sea as part and parcel of the job. Looking back now, one can see that it was a hard and dangerous life, one where many a brave fisherman lost their lives in the process. Some were even friends of mine who never got out of their teens, never had children or families – they didn't get the opportunity.'

What happens when there is illness on board a trawler? It can be a nightmare, as the example of the Grimsby trawler *Northern Jewel* reveals. The vessel returned to Grimsby Fish Docks on the unlikely date of 29th February 1956 with a good catch of 2,850 kits. She had

Anyone want to buy a fish? The calm before the auction storm at Grimsby. Believe it or not every single one of these thousands of fish would have been snapped up and distributed to processors, restaurants, fishmongers and, of course, fish and chip shops all over Britain.

been fishing off the Norwegian coast and had been away for just under three weeks, but what an eventful 20 days it had been, as skipper Tregunno told the newspaper at the time. The problem was that there had been a flu epidemic on board, just what you do not need when you are fishing off the Scandinavian coast during one of the coldest spells of the winter.

'The radio operator, Jack Douglas, and I were the only ones to escape,' the skipper reported. 'Even the cook caught it but he never missed cooking a meal for the rest of us. We had it all the time we were fishing, first one man and then another going down with it. The men were staggering about on deck but they kept working. I used up all the influenza mixture in the medicine chest and then I started giving them a glass of rum, three or four aspirins and sending them below for six hours. We were always a man or two short on deck but everyone was splendid.

'If the men had reported sick I should just have had to lie to. It would not have been any use going into harbour as we should only have been put into quarantine. I was proud to command such a fine crew.'

The owner of the *Northern Jewel*, John Bennett of Northern Trawlers Ltd, added his own tribute and summed it all up when he said: 'Fishermen are the only men living who would do such a thing.'

Tales of tragedy and near tragedy have abounded for as long as there have been people willing to take the risk of picking up the gauntlet thrown down by the ocean and bringing home the fish.

More than a century ago, in 1889 when Queen Victoria still reigned supreme, Lincolnshire was enjoying a fishing boom and there were many reaping the benefit. In Grimsby one such man was George Clifford, who enjoyed having regular work as a deckhand. He only earned about £1 a week and had a wife and family to keep but low though the wage was, he was still able to hand over housekeeping regularly.

George decided he wanted the rare treat of Christmas at home with his family and that was exactly how things were shaping until there came a visitor asking him to join the crew of the *Sando* for a trip. George refused until the offer of an instant half sovereign, a pound of tobacco and a bottle of whisky changed his mind.

'As we were going out of the dock the skipper heard of a ship that had landed what was a record £500 worth of fish from Iceland. He had high hopes of doing the same and we were all in good spirits because that would have meant a good pay packet for all of us. So we headed for the Faroes with smiles on our faces even though there was a very cold and strong wind blowing. The sea was rough and it was a bit of a battle getting to the fishing grounds but we got there and the skipper didn't waste any time in getting to work. We had the nets out for three hours without catching a thing and the skipper was impatient. He didn't see any point in hanging around and told us that we were going to Iceland instead. So, with the weather getting worse we hauled in the nets and headed north.

'Off to Iceland we went in a raging gale. How we ever got there in that gale I'll never know. It was snowing, blowing and freezing. It was really very cold. When we arrived off Iceland it was too rough to fish. We had tried to put in at a fjord for shelter but then when we tried to get out again we couldn't make it. We were beaten back each time. The seas were mountainous and we were there for three days.

'We eventually got out and started to fish but it was hopeless. The wind blew terribly and the sea tossed us about like a cork. We tried to get back to the fjord but we couldn't. We struggled and fought with that sea but it was no use and we could not secure shelter. We shipped sea upon sea and almost turned over. It was still snowing and freezing and we couldn't see anything. We desperately tried to reach that fjord again but all in vain. We had shipped so much water that the ship was at a perilous angle. All at once she shipped a proper broadside which swept away the wheelhouse, compass and all. I thought that was the end.

'The weather showed no mercy and heavy seas continued to smash over the vessel as she fought to survive, helpless in a storm of terrifying intensity. She rolled, pitched and heaved with her crew, like herself, fighting for their lives. We had to chop away our gear or we would certainly have gone down. One poor chap by the name of William Brown had his head cut clean from his shoulders and his body was washed overboard. We had to cling to anything we could to avoid being swept away too.

'We had to do something and do it quickly so we tried to pump out the engine room which had filled with water. We found that the pumps were choked and the plates had shifted so we started to bale out with buckets passing along a chain from one to another. The water was actually quite warm in the engine room but it was still bitterly cold outside and eventually the man at the top of the chain collapsed because of that cold. We put him in the warm water to bring him round and unfreeze him. Another man took his place and the same thing happened to him. It went on like that all through the night. We were all dead beat the next day and we had no food or anything to warm us up a little.

'There was no chance of us resting because that would have been the end of us. We had to keep going to survive and we had to get the engine to restart. We were all battered and bruised and it was a relief when we managed to get the pumps going again. It made no difference to our situation but we felt that there was some hope at least even though the storm was still raging and we were in dire straits.

'We had nothing to help us keep going, not even light but we knew that our survival was in our own hands. We were all experienced seamen and we knew that we had to try and keep her facing into the wind so we were surprised when the skipper suddenly told us that he was going to bring her about and let her run with the wind. The crew erupted in opposition and the mate, Bill Harris, who had been through a similar experience and seen the ship lost, voiced his opinion that we would never seen Grimsby again if the skipper took such an action. The skipper was not to be argued with though and he reminded everyone that he was the master of the ship and would do as he decided.

'So we went along with it and he turned her round. Now we were still being tossed around but didn't know where the wind was driving us. It looked very grim and in a final act of desperation the skipper blew one long blast on the whistle in the hope that someone, somewhere might hear. It resulted in something of a miracle. We were nearer the Icelandic shore than we realised and some villagers heard us. They immediately put out to find us and when they did they saw that we were no longer in any fit state to do any more for ourselves. Even our clothes were frozen to us. They treated us to get us warmer and took charge of the vessel. Then they took us ashore and looked after us.

'We all wrote letters home but this was a remote part of Iceland and no word reached Grimsby for two months. In the meantime we had been written off, insurance money had been paid and one woman who thought she was a widow even remarried.'

One woman who refused to give up was George's wife, who was pitied by many who thought she was in denial. She always maintained though that her husband would return and she even declined to accept the insurance money because of her strong belief.

'The owners sent the *Sando*'s sister ship, the *Sudero*, to escort us back,' said George. 'Sufficient repairs had been made but we took our time and eventually arrived back months later than expected. A vast crowd lined the docks to greet us and we were all wiser men when we set foot on the Grimsby harbour once again.'

There are many such memories although it is sad to note that too many fishermen have taken their stories with them, their tales not having a happy ending. Fishermen have regularly embraced tragedy, worked in horrendous conditions and revealed a certain kind of character that refuses to be beaten either by odds or elements.

So, what is it like to be on board a fishing boat? Tough – really tough.

┌─────────────────┐

Chapter 7

Fishing, Football and Cats

It seems perfectly logical that a trawler based at Grimsby would have the name *Grimsby Town*, to celebrate the links between local fishing and football. Every vessel needs a name and there are only so many 'Princess Rose' or 'Deep Sea Diana' titles to hand round. Clearly, too, there are similarities between footballers and fishermen since they are both trying to get something into the net. However, it did not begin or end there by any means.

Consolidated Fisheries Ltd owned the famous 'football fleet' and it all began in 1933 when it was decided that GY505, a 150-ton net trawler built at Smiths Dock in Middlesbrough, should be named *Arsenal* after the club which was so dominant at the time under the management of legendary boss Herbert Chapman. The idea gained strength and the hugely successful company decreed that all of its new vessels would be named after then First Division football clubs.

The *Arsenal* set out on its maiden fishing voyage at the beginning of August 1933 and returned 21 days later with the first repayment of Consolidated Fisheries' investment – 1,250 boxes of fish, which had a gross value of just under £945. Many such successful trips were undertaken during the years that followed although the vessel did have its ups and downs. It was bought by the Admiralty in 1939, who paid £22,420 with the intention of the *Arsenal* becoming an anti-submarine vessel. Sadly, that was to cause the end of the ship since in mid-November 1940 she collided with a Polish destroyer in the River Clyde estuary and sank. She remains there to this day.

Another *Arsenal* took to the water towards the end of September 1957 and made its maiden trip to Iceland in mid-February 1958. The ship experienced crew problems, Icelandic problems and repair problems but it kept going and kept on bringing home fish until making a final trip to the scrapyard in March 1975.

The Arsenal *was one of the best known of the Consolidated Fisheries football fleet. This is* Arsenal 2, *launched in 1957 after the first* Arsenal *sank in 1940, following a collision with a Polish destroyer.*

The steam trawler Grimsby Town *which was built in 1934.*
(An original painting by Steve Farrow)

During the years after the original *Arsenal* first slipped onto the water, Consolidated Fisheries Ltd were as good as their word and added many other names to their famous football fleet. *Grimsby Town* was also built at Smiths Dock in Middlesbrough but a year later than the *Arsenal* in 1934. GY81 was a 160-ton vessel and was named in premature celebration of the Grimsby Town football club's much anticipated promotion to the First Division. She was launched in July 1934 and greeted in Grimsby the following day in party fashion, with local dignitaries including Grimsby Town players welcoming the new trawler. Within two days she embarked on her maiden fishing trip to Icelandic waters and returned 19 days later with a catch of 1,250 boxes of fish yielding almost £1,438.

The *Grimsby Town* must be one of the few vessels ever to have officially opened something, but that was what happened on 4th October 1934 when she performed the celebratory duty for the new

Fish Dock No 3 by sailing into the dock and thus cutting a ribbon at the same time. With many successful fishing trips and a lot of publicity, the *Grimsby Town* became something of a local celebrity and there were many who were not keen to see her go when she, too, was bought by the Admiralty for just under £24,000 in August 1939 and put into service as an anti-submarine vessel.

Despite being busy throughout the world, the *Grimsby Town* survived the war and was sold to the Hill Ice Company in January 1946. Ironically and tragically she ran aground just three months later in Iceland, with three men killed. Several attempts were made to refloat her but they all failed and salvage proved to be the only answer.

That was not the end of the tale though, since on 19th November 1952 another *Grimsby Town* was launched. GY246 was built by Cochrane's of Selby and was almost half as big again as her predecessor. Her maiden trip was on 28th July 1953 and she brought back 1,608 kits of fish yielding £4,560. Everyone concerned was delighted but there was less delight when a few years later she ran foul of Icelandic boats during the Cod Wars. That aside she proved to be an excellent vessel and a success story for her owners until late March 1975 when she set sail for the last time – to the breakers yard.

The *Aston Villa*, GY508 was sister ship to the original *Arsenal*. Her maiden voyage was on 12th August 1933 and when she returned 18 days later she landed about 1,200 kits at Grimsby. This was worth a little more than £607 which was an encouraging start. There was an early intervention in *Aston Villa*'s career when the Admiralty decided to buy her in July 1936. However, she continued to fish and in 1947 she was bought by Boston Deep Sea Fishing Co Ltd, who kept her until 1953 under the new name of *Fotherby*. Another name change occurred in 1953 when she was sold again, this time to a Polish company who renamed her *Pollux*.

Just to confuse matters, another *Aston Villa* was commissioned and with her GY428 registration number newly-painted she sailed on her maiden voyage to Bear Island on 7th September 1937. Almost exactly two years later she was requisitioned by the Admiralty and joined the ranks of other trawlers put to work as anti-submarine vessels. In May 1940 she met her end following an attack by enemy aircraft. She sank, and thus ended the Aston Villa saga – or did it? In 1946 the vessel known as *Anthony Hope* – its second name – was bought by Consolidated Fisheries in 1957 and renamed the *Aston Villa*, this becoming the third vessel with that distinctive name. This version was GY42 and fared quite well until May 1965 when it was scrapped, bringing to a close an era of Aston Villa ruling the high seas.

And, how about the story of the *Barnsley* which was once the *Burnley*? The vessel was being built at Goole for Consolidated Fisheries in 1960 and was called the *Burnley* before it was launched as the *Barnsley*. Having enjoyed a maiden trip in late October 1960, the boat went on to create several new catch records as well as experiencing a few dramas from stowaway to suicide, and dismissal from fishing grounds by Russian warships. In July 1978, after bringing home £210,000 of fish from six trips thus far that year, the ship was sold to Colne Shipping in Lowestoft. Two years later she became an oil rig supply vessel and two years after that she was finally scrapped, an undignified end for a vessel that had really ridden along on the crest of a wave.

Talking of the crest of a wave, Blackburn Rovers were enjoying a great spell on the pitch when the new vessel bearing that famous name was launched on 8th November 1934 and made her maiden trip exactly a month later. She had her challenges during the next few years including twice falling foul of extreme weather, but she remained in sufficiently good shape to join those other trawlers requisitioned by the Admiralty in 1939 for anti-submarine work. That is really where her story ends since the following year she was lost somewhere in the North Sea, destroyed by either a mine or a U-boat. Her fate has never been made clear.

However, another *Blackburn Rovers* was built and launched in September 1962. She lasted much longer and had a change of career in 1981 when she was converted for oil rig duties. She even had a change of nationality in the latter part of 1987 when she was bought by a fishing company in Cyprus and had her name changed to *Giant Fish*.

The *Carlisle* was another of the football fleet. She was launched in 1961 and had quite an interesting career, including breaking a landing record when she brought home 2,563 kits from Icelandic waters in July 1974, a catch which yielded £32,000, a record for her size of vessel. Needless to say, the *Carlisle* ran into trouble during the Cod War but she survived to tell the tale and later was converted, first for sand eel fishing and then for oil rig supplies. The latter was in August 1980 and she served well until July 1987 when she made her final voyage to the scrapyard after 26 years of active life.

Next we come to the *Mareham*, which was launched in June 1937 and managed to bump into the south quay as she entered Grimsby dock for the first time two months later. In just a few days she set off on her maiden voyage under skipper Robert Harris. Hang on a minute, I hear you think, how come the *Mareham* is considered to be one of the football fleet? Well, in December 1938 her name was changed to *Coventry City*. She had an interesting career after that. She was requisitioned in 1939 for duty as an anti-submarine vessel and was loaned to the US Navy in 1942. She patrolled American waters until October of that year, when she was sent to South Africa until the war ended and she returned to fishing in August 1945. Throughout her life, *Coventry City* had a reputation for being rather accident-prone, but she survived to complete 26 years of service until being scrapped in June 1964.

Crystal Palace was one of the later ships of the football fleet, having been launched in November 1961 and started her maiden voyage to Iceland in January 1962. She was quite a successful trawler despite being another of those caught up in the Cod War. For a time she was refitted as a fishing research vessel and then in March 1981 joined the useful ranks of the oil rig supply vessels among which she performed admirably until 1992, when she was finally scrapped in the Medway.

The *Derby County*'s maiden trip in late August 1933 was to Iceland and hit a problem as soon as she arrived. The winch was faulty and could not handle deep sea work. The skipper sent a telegram to explain the problem and proposed that he fish in shallow water instead. In the event, he did just that and landed 1,250 boxes of fish before the *Derby County* went for repairs. So much for the first trip, but the second trip also presented problems with a faulty suction feed pipe. The problem was repaired in Iceland and the vessel returned to work. The Admiralty paid £22,518 for her to become an anti-submarine vessel in August 1939 and she served valiantly until returning to fishing in 1945, after which she continued to fish until being scrapped in Belgium in February 1964.

Everton Football Club sent a telegram of good wishes when their namesake vessel left for her maiden voyage in September 1958 and she certainly enjoyed a bright start to her fishing career. She proved to be an excellent fishing vessel despite the usual repairs and problems which are common to all engaged in the industry. She was fired upon and suffered a little damage during the confrontation with Iceland in the 1970s but the *Everton* shrugged this off and continued until March 1975. At one stage it seemed that she was set to become a tourist attraction but that idea was scrapped, which was the same fate as that suffered by the *Everton* herself in March 1976.

The *Gillingham*'s maiden voyage was in January 1960 and she fished well until 1981 when she was converted to a supply vessel for the oil rigs. During her fishing years, though, she claimed an amazing record in December 1975 when she landed 1,759 kits which yielded £54,785. This had never before been accomplished by a vessel of her size. Sadly, she was scrapped in July 1987 but she certainly made her mark when she was around.

Huddersfield Town was another of the early ships in the fishing fleet, having been launched on 21st August 1933 and put into service in October of that year. It was decided that her name was too long and permission was sought to drop the *Town* part. Having at first been granted, permission was then withdrawn because it was considered that *Huddersfield* alone did not convey the football connection. That is by no means the end of the name saga, though. The ship served well, was called up for national duty in 1939, as yet another anti-submarine vessel, and then returned to civvy street in 1945, when she resumed fishing. It came as a surprise in July 1962 when permission was granted to change her name and the *Huddersfield Town* became the *Leeds United*! It must have seemed hardly worth the trouble, since after being sold to Boston Deep Sea Fishing Co Ltd in June 1963 she was scrapped in Holland just a few months later.

Then came another *Huddersfield Town*, which went on her maiden voyage in January 1963. She proved to be an extremely successful vessel and more than earned her keep. In July 1978 she was sold to Colne Shipping of Lowestoft but had already brought home £216,000 of fish from her five trips that year. In December 1981 she followed in the wake of many others when she was converted to an oil rig supply vessel and in January 1992 she was finally sent to the breaker's yard, thus ending a memorable lifespan.

Perhaps we should mention *Hull City* even though that particular football team has always been seen as Grimsby's chief rival. She took to the water at the start of 1953 and was given a warm welcome when she arrived in Grimsby for the first time. She lived through the tense times of antagonism with Iceland and the depression in fish sales and even once had the indignity, in June 1969, of being towed by *Grimsby Town* when her trawl tangled in her propeller. She was eventually scrapped in June 1975.

The *Carmarthen Castle* – GY62 – went on her maiden voyage in November 1933 and landed a reasonable catch worth £950. Of course, there was no Carmarthen Castle United or Wanderers but there was a Leeds United and that is why in May 1934 she was renamed. She was bought by the Admiralty for £22,175 in September 1939 and for nearly seven years *Leeds United* served as an auxiliary patrol vessel before new owners bought her and she fished out of Hull. About 20 months later in November 1947 Consolidated bought her again and once more she was a Grimsby vessel – GY386. She stayed that way until an appointment with the scrapyard in April 1962.

Leicester City began life in the 1930s and was keenly followed by the football club, its players and fans. She served as an anti-submarine vessel during the war and came through it but in March 1953 she met her end in tragic circumstances. One night she was caught in a storm near the Isle of Hoy in the Orkneys and ran aground. The crew had abandoned ship but their lifeboat capsized and seven lives were lost, although the Stromness lifeboat saved four others.

The *Pembroke Castle* started life with a non-football name in October 1933, the tenth vessel to be built for Consolidated Fisheries by Smiths Dock of Middlesbrough. After nearly five years of near-exemplary service she was adopted into the fishing fleet in April 1938 and renamed *Lincoln City*. What should have been a long and successful career was prematurely ended on 21st February 1941. *Lincoln City* had become an anti-submarine vessel for the war effort and all had been going well until she was caught by enemy aircraft fire off the coast of the Faroe Islands and suffered sufficient damage to sink her.

There had to be another *Lincoln City* and therefore the requisitioned *Cape Warwick* had a change of name at the end of the war. She served well and faced up to Icelandic gunboats more than once during the Cod War. She was eventually scrapped in Holland in September 1963.

Launched in October 1933, the *Barry Castle* was also destined for a name change and on 31st May 1934 she officially became *Manchester City* – but was not heading for a champagne career. Requisitioned in

January 1940, she was on patrol in the English Channel when she struck a mine near Dover and was instantly sunk.

The *Norwich City* fared rather better. Completed in 1938, she went to work for Consolidated Fisheries before becoming an anti-submarine vessel in September 1939. She was loaned to the US Navy in 1942 and saw out her war years as an escort vessel in South Africa. Returning to her fishing career, she remained successfully in service until being scrapped in June 1964.

Notts County heralded a slight change in policy when she was named in 1937, the first of the fishing fleet to be named after a non-Division One team. That was not her only claim to fame either. Within two months of arriving at Grimsby for the first time she had hit both the coping stone of the Royal Dock and another vessel. When it came to bringing home the fish, though, the *Notts County* was pretty good and it was with some reluctance that she was sold to the Admiralty for anti-submarine work in September 1939. Sadly that proved to be her undoing as she was destroyed in March 1942 after being torpedoed by a U-boat.

However, 18 years later another *Notts County* was launched, which after several years of excellent service ran aground in Isafjord Bay, Iceland in February 1968 and her crew had to be rescued. All but one survived, and he was Robert Bowie who died from water exposure. After several attempts the vessel was finally refloated but was considered too damaged to be anything but a write-off. A local businessman paid just £35 for her and that was the end of the second *Notts County*.

Nottingham Forest have always been rather touchy about the name of their club and hated being called 'Notts Forest', but that was the title put on the newest of the football fleet in September 1960 when she was launched. It certainly did her no harm. The *Notts Forest* successfully lived through the Cod War, strikes and various other escapades and brought home many excellent catches worth more than £50,000 a time. In January 1978 she was sold to Colne Shipping of

Lowestoft and continued fishing for a while before becoming a tourist attraction at the resort. In 1981 she was converted to a supply vessel for oil rigs and kept going until the very end of 1991 when she slipped quietly away to the breaker's yard after 31 years of service.

The *Port Vale* had a similarly long life, having started out in 1957 and kept busy until going for scrap in 1987. She also lived through several adventures including the Cod War and even being grounded, though only slightly damaged. She was game all the way through and consistently brought back a vessel load of fish. For the last six years of her life she was also a supply vessel for the oil rigs, a comparatively easy task, suitable for a lady in semi-retirement.

The *Preston North End* was launched in 1934 and became something of a film star. Scenes for the late 1930s film *The Last Adventure* were filmed aboard her and many fishing folk made a special trip to the local picture house to see her on the big screen when it was on general release. Not long afterwards she was signed up by the Admiralty and survived the war, returning to fishing in 1945. Sadly she ran aground in terrible weather conditions on Geirfugladranger Reef, Iceland, and a major rescue mission was launched. Unfortunately not all the crew survived and the *Preston North End* herself was written off, a sad end for a movie star trawler.

The *Sheffield Wednesday* was another of those early football fleet vessels, having been launched in 1933, and was just getting into stride when in June 1937 she was sold to a Dutch firm and renamed *Erin*. She also found herself being requisitioned by the Admiralty in 1940 and served for nearly two years before an explosion sank her in Gibraltar Bay in January 1942.

What about Spurs? A new vessel with that name joined the football fleet in August 1933 and after several adventures became an Admiralty ship in September 1939. Not even being bombed in June 1940 when she was part of the Dunkirk rescue flotilla, put *Spurs* out of permanent action and she returned to her fishing activities in 1946. She even ran aground a couple of times but still returned to work and it was with a lot of sadness that this gutsy lady was finally sent for scrap in April 1962.

That is not the end of the story, however, since another *Spurs* was launched in 1962 and made it through the Cod War, fires, crew problems and various excitements, even finding time to bring back some record landings. She was finally scrapped in July 1991 but certainly kept the Spurs flag flying high until then.

Stoke City had an interesting life which began in 1935 and ended at the scrapyard in 1964. She did her bit during the war and was another of those trawlers which lived through various ups and downs but always brought back a healthy landing.

Wolves had a strange start to life because she was originally known as *Jean Eva* when she was launched in December 1934. It was not until after several successful fishing trips and the loss of two men in separate incidents that she became known as *Wolves* in April 1938. Of course she was signed up by the Admiralty, and spent the war years as a patrol vessel before returning to fishing in 1945. During her time with the Admiralty she was bought by a company called Crampins who later sold her to another owner in 1947, whereupon she experienced another name change and became the *Pataudi*. She continued working until May 1961 when she was scrapped.

That was not quite the end of the story, since another ship was launched in 1946 as the *St Matthew*. However, when Consolidated Fisheries paid £70,000 for her on 1st January 1957 they changed her name to *Wolverhampton Wanderers,* which must have had the signwriter rubbing his hands with delight since it was the longest name ever seen on a British trawler. She was a fairly resilient vessel and was none the worse for running aground several times. She started to go downhill a little in the mid-1960s and was tied up and left for almost a year before finally going for scrap in June 1967. Although she was officially known as *Wolverhampton Wanderers* everyone knew her as *Wolves*, and she proved to be a good follow-up to her predecessor.

Built in 1933, the *Dynvor Castle* became a member of the football fleet in 1938 when she was renamed *York City*. A patrol vessel during the war, *York City* was also arrested twice in peacetime, once by the Russians and once by the Icelandic navy. She also rescued a German crew from their sinking ship in September 1956, so *York City* had a far from boring life before she was scrapped in February 1964.

That just about covers all the vessels of the famous football fleet. Well, almost. There is one other which has been deliberately left until last. This trawler was launched in June 1961 and was unique as it was the only member of the football fleet to be named after a foreign club. As a gesture of goodwill the football club presented a pennant to trawler owners Consolidated Fisheries, which is why in the company's boardroom all visitors could see prominently displayed the name *Real Madrid*. The vessel was on the front line in the Cod War and had quite a few altercations with the Icelandic authorities but the various skippers never once flinched. The vessel herself ran aground more than once, had a fire and various other incidents but lasted until being scrapped in January 1981.

The football fleet is fondly remembered by the fishing fraternity and has carved its own niche in the record books. The final whistle might have been blown on those great vessels but they are still playing extra time in the history of the Lincolnshire fishing industry.

Yet the football fleet is not the only 'family' known to the industry. There was also the famous 'cat class', whose story started in 1957 when the Ross Group took delivery of a new vessel at Grimsby. That new vessel did not have a name at first and heads were being scratched when someone came up with the bright idea of asking schoolchildren to help. Other vessels of the same specification were also being built or planned so the more names the merrier.

So Grimsby schoolchildren were asked to think up ideas for the new vessels, their only restriction being that they had to have a theme, preferably the cat family. The children were inspired

The Ross Tiger *on the slipway. She was launched in 1957 and served well before avoiding the scrapyard by becoming such a popular visitor attraction. She could tell a few tales of life in the trawling industry.*

because there were twelve new vessels and it was a rare honour to be asked to name them.

In the event the children came up with an excellent list, even though some of the cats seemed to have strayed a little. One even became a zebra, because a little girl could not think of a cat name that was different from the others already listed. The Ross directors decided that, since she had put her heart and soul into searching for a cat, they would indeed allow 'zebra' into their cat class, especially since someone else had come up with 'jackal' which was not exactly feline either.

The *Ross Tiger* was launched in February 1957 amid a blaze of publicity and she certainly lived up to her name, as she served well for more than a quarter of a century and brought back many worthy catches before becoming an oil-rig supply vessel for seven years for Cam Shipping. And she is still around today, which pleases nobody more than John Vincent of the National Fishing Heritage Centre at Grimsby.

'I worked on her when I was at sea,' said John. 'We had many great trips and experiences together and now she is permanently moored at the Heritage Centre and I see her every day as well as taking guided tours around her. I still get a thrill every time I step on board. The *Ross Tiger* was the first of her kind, she was beautiful and the most modern in technology of her age. She was originally a double-sided trawler which meant you could fish from either side and she was certainly good at her job. She underwent some changes around 1967 because that ability was no longer needed.

The Ross Jaguar *at sea. This is another of the popular 'Cat' fleet, named by Grimsby schoolchildren in the 1950s.*

'You know, you always build a relationship with the vessel you are on and I have to say that she still means a lot to me. Her fishing gear was taken off when she became a supply vessel but bit by bit she has been restored to her former glory. She would have been in the scrapyard long before now but for the generosity of Cam Shipping who handed her over to the council for the sum of £1 knowing that she was going to become part of the Fishing Heritage Centre. I was delighted when I heard about it and she is there now for all to see.

Other members of the 'cat family' followed in quick order. Following the success of the *Ross Tiger* came the *Ross Leopard* in October 1957. Two months later the *Ross Jaguar* took to the sea. In April 1958 both the *Ross Panther* and the *Ross Cougar* were launched and then there was a gap until November 1959 when the *Ross Cheetah* appeared.

The first half-dozen vessels were all put to work straight away but there were more to come, all in 1960. First came the *Ross Lynx* in February, followed two months later by the *Ross Jackal* and then in August the *Ross Puma*, which was a little bit of a cheat since the puma and the cougar are different names for the same animal. In October there was another double celebration as the *Ross Genet* and the *Ross Civet* were both launched and the following month the last, but by no means the least, was moored in Grimsby. Yes, the *Ross Zebra* had earned her stripes.

These vessels all served well and had a full life, including experiencing the hostilities with Iceland. Only one did not go the distance, the *Ross Puma*. She was unfortunately wrecked beyond repair in April 1968 when she ran foul of bad weather at Hoy in the Pentland Firth.

There was also a *Ross Lion* but she was not of the same specification and therefore was not considered to be among the 'cat class family' in anything other than name.

The 'cats' worked hard and successfully but the demise of the fishing industry took its toll on them and they mostly found work in other jobs, as did the *Ross Tiger*. The last of them to bring home a catch was the *Ross Cougar* in the summer of 1985.

The Boston Fury *heralded a new design in trawlers in the mid-1950s. Hard to believe that this was state-of-the-art trawling in its day.*

Those schoolchildren who named the Ross cat class will have grown-up children of their own by now and possibly even grandchildren, but it must be good to know that they can still find a piece of their own history moored for all to see in Grimsby.

With the many thousands of fishing vessels which have been registered to Lincolnshire's ports over the years it is fascinating that those which have caught the imagination more than any others are the football family and the cat class. Let us not forget all the others though, among them the *Boston Fury*, the *Ross Daring* and the *Defiance* which show such strength of character in their names, or indeed the *Ross Delight*, the *Rigoletto* or the *Loyal* which somehow convey other qualities of life.

Perhaps we read too much into names, but even in the heat of the moment the Icelandic gunboats were not keen to tackle the might of the *Ross Tiger*!

Chapter 8

Surprises on Board

Countless fishing voyages have gone exactly to plan and everyone has returned home safely and happy, content with a decent catch to show for their hard work. However, there are many other voyages which have surprises and tales of the unexpected to report.

We have all heard yarns of the 'one that got away' but those stories are not confined to the exaggerated memoirs of sporting fishing fellows. Ancient fishing mariners also all have a tale to tell of the things they have seen and nearly caught. These are tales that have crossed-legged youngsters sitting in total silence with widening eyes and dropping lower jaws – grown-ups too! In many cases the one that got away didn't and there are plenty of eye witnesses to testify that a large shark or octopus had indeed invited itself to come home to dear old blighty.

All kinds of things have been hauled up during the centuries of trawling but now and again there is something different, something

Tales of the unexpected! A worthy trawlerman displays the monk fish they neither expected nor wanted to find in their nets. Hope it doesn't mind ash dropping on its head!

that hits the headlines. Seals are quite commonly caught in nets and in most cases every effort is made to safely release them. It is certain to happen since the hunting seal comes across what appears to him to be an underwater supermarket. You can't blame him for trying a little shoplifting.

Turtles are also fairly common, especially when they are following fleets of jellyfish upon which many of them feed. It is said that climate change has caused more jellyfish to be found in British waters and therefore more turtles on excursion from the Mediterranean. That is a debate for the politicians, however. The fact remains that our fishing men do have close encounters with turtles during the course of their work.

Conger eels also find their way into the nets and now and then a real whopper is brought ashore, like the one caught some years ago. It weighed in at 123 lbs – nearly 60 kilos if you prefer – and was about eight feet in length. You wouldn't have wanted to meet up with him while you were scuba diving even though he would probably have ignored you. Still, he was a surprise package when the nets were hauled aboard on the North Sea.

The conger is dwarfed by basking sharks and they have been known to be brought home to Grimsby. We are talking about 100 stone or more of huge fish and a good many shark steaks. It must be said that trawlermen do not deliberately set out to catch fish like these and are as surprised as everyone else when they turn up in the net. The basking shark is pretty harmless despite its size but occasionally a shark with teeth and attitude comes aboard, especially from fishing grounds off Scotland. They, of course, are handled very carefully. Sightings of whales and dolphins are not at all uncommon and small species have been known to get tangled in the nets. Even an occasional walrus has been seen as ships venture further north.

If a sturgeon is landed – and some of them can be pretty big at 20 ft and 1,000 lbs – the crew know where it will possibly be heading, since by tradition it must first be offered to the reigning monarch. If the Queen declines then it is put up for offers on the open market. It is a rare sight at a Lincolnshire fishing port but a few have been landed during the years.

Surprises at sea and events for the captain's log are not confined to unusual sightings and landings. Quite regularly there have been unexpected problems involving the crew. The history of the 'football fleet' reveals all kinds of events.

Some things just make you go 'Ouch!' In April 1939 the *Huddersfield Town* was just leaving the dock when novice deckhand Norman Piggott caught his foot in the steering gear. Yes, his whole foot was crushed and most of the ball of his foot was torn away. Are your eyes watering? He was put back on land immediately and taken to hospital where most of him recovered.

In December 1963 the second *Arsenal* was 50 miles off the coast of north Scotland when a fire broke out and skipper Bill Hardie had to send a distress call. It was a dramatic scene as the 19-man crew put into operation the fire drill they had been trained on for every trip. Some were injured or overcome by smoke but after five hours they put out the blaze and the captain was able to send out another radio call to say that everything was under control. He congratulated his crew and headed for shore for repairs to the gutted quarters.

The annals of court cases are absolutely full of stories of crew members being fined for being a 'disobedient fisherman'. Mostly this was about men who had refused to sail with their vessel or had actually jumped off just as the ship was leaving the port. With crews kept to a minimum every pair of hands was needed so the last-minute loss of a man was bad news.

Sometimes vessels have found themselves with an extra man. In January 1976 the *Barnsley* set sail to the White Sea fishing grounds not knowing there was a stowaway on board. Royce Rothenberg was just 15 at the time and his love of the sea got the better of him. However, when Royce surprised the crew by being found aboard, skipper George Turrell had no alternative but to head for the nearest port in Scotland – Peterhead – and drop him off for a land trip back to Grimsby. Needless to say, the young man was not at all popular as he had cost both time and money.

In November 1963 a crew member of the *Gillingham* was fined £1 and ordered to pay costs of £2 2s when he refused to sail with the vessel because the cook was ill and he feared infection. There was worse to come on board the *Gillingham*, however. In July 1971 she was leaving the dock when a major incident erupted. A crew member leaped onto the quay but was then seen back on board and covered in blood. That man and another then attacked a further crew member and later attacked the cook. Both victims were badly hurt and the skipper had no choice but to return to Grimsby. The two attackers,

Graham Horsfall and Jim Padgett were later sent to prison for eighteen months each, with the judge refusing to take into account that when both men pleaded guilty they explained that they had been drinking heavily.

Drink was always a problem – some things never change. In January 1975, the *Aldershot* was forced to put into Iceland after heavy seas had caused some damage. During the stay for repairs five crew members had a bit too much to drink and went on the rampage on board, throwing cooking utensils and other equipment overboard before they were brought under control. The skipper was not impressed and neither were the Grimsby magistrates, who handed out suspended sentences and heavy fines to those involved.

Just over a year later the *Aldershot* was involved in another incident. Skipper Dave Ferrand put out to sea on 20th May 1976 but was forced to radio for help when he discovered that the automatic steering gear had been damaged with an axe. He returned to Grimsby where a team of police officers met the vessel and took the entire crew of 18 to the police station. The culprits were eventually revealed.

The captain of the second *Arsenal* in October 1970, Joe Harris, had an incident on his hands when Icelandic police boarded his ship while she was moored in Seydisfjord for engine repairs. There had been a complaint of thefts from local ships and unruly conduct. The captain cooperated with the police but defended his men. Eventually five of his men confessed to the allegations. The local court found four of the men guilty, gave suspended jail sentences to them and fined them. The trawler owners paid the fines and recouped them later. It was another interesting episode in the life of Joe Harris.

Quite often, thefts have taken place from the fishing vessel herself and once again there are many court records of such incidents. The watchman of the *Barnsley* pleaded guilty in April 1964 to the theft of peas and margarine, which were valued at a little under 4s (20p). He was fined £3, so typical of the pointlessness of such crime.

Incidents involving mutinous crew and dramas on board can weigh heavily on the skipper, whose burden is already great. Even then, they do not weigh as heavily as the untimely death of a crew member, especially one lost overboard. In September 1935 the *Arsenal* was fishing near Bear Island when deckie Ray Goss slipped into the water while trying to fix a rope. The 20-year-old was thrown a rope by the mate and some other crew members and he looked as if he was going to make it back onto the boat. However, as he neared safety he lost his grip on the rope, probably because his fingers were numb. He fell back into the ocean and was never seen again.

Sometimes illness strikes a very serious note. The mate of the *Port Vale*, Herbert Johnson, was taken ill in August 1963 with suspected appendicitis. The vessel headed for the nearest port and succeeded in getting him to hospital in Siglufjord. Meanwhile, Consolidated Fisheries, the owners, arranged for his wife to be flown to be with him and she was at his side when he died of suspected peritonitis.

There are sometimes happier endings and tales of heroism to report. The second *Grimsby Town* was fishing in the Barents Sea in December 1965 when the net was suddenly yanked further out by the weather, and deckhand Neil Bray was pulled into the sea with it. The third hand, Fred Hopwood, flung his oilskins to one side and jumped overboard to the rescue. He managed to grab hold of Bray and haul him to the ship where he clung onto the net until the crew could drag both men back on board. It was a remarkable action by Hopwood who did not hesitate to go to the rescue even though he was himself a non-swimmer. His courage was recognised later when he was awarded the Royal Humane Society's bronze medal and certificate.

Strange creatures appear in their nets but skippers remain unflustered. Crew are arrested for theft and assault, there are fires on board, thick fogs to contend with and various bumps and collisions with other vessels and quays, not to mention running aground. There are fights on board and men taken seriously ill or sometimes lost overboard.

One thing is certain – the captain's log does not make for boring reading!

Chapter 9

Things to Learn

If you know nothing about the industry of fishing you can be excused for being baffled as experienced seamen around you seem to be speaking a different language. There is a word for everything and everything has its word, but those words can vary a great deal from port to port. As an example, the person given the job of unloading the kits or boxes of fish is known as a 'lumper' in Grimsby but a 'bobber' in Hull, apparently because of the need to bob down when working. So for the uninitiated, here are some terms with which to become familiar so that you can at least be able to find your way around the vessel.

The *wheelhouse* is the brains of the ship, the very nerve centre from which all the important decisions are taken.

The *radio room* is what it says. This is the mouth of the vessel and capable of radio communication to and from shore and with other vessels. There is a morse communication system too – just in case.

The *engine room,* which was also once called the *boiler room,* does indeed house the engine. Now usually diesel or oil-fired, once of course it was coal-fired which meant a lot of hard work and a lot of heat, just the place to be when you were travelling through icy Arctic waters.

The *binnacle* has the job of housing the vessel's compass, usually viewed through mirrors from the bridge.

The *coal store* is now mostly a thing of the past and has given way to more fish storage. It used to have an important role to play as the boiler's personal larder, full when the trip started but often perilously empty by the time the ship was in sight of the coast again.

The *anchor winch* might seem to be pretty self explanatory but more than one apprentice has been told to pull up the anchor by hand or, even better, to find the scales to weigh anchor. Winches made the back-breaking job of hauling up the anchor much easier and when they became auto-operated many a seaman rejoiced.

The *radar scanner* might be confused with a high-powered self-adjusting television aerial but it does of course link to the radar screen in the bridge and has been an essential part of the fishing vessel's equipment from the day it was invented.

The *steam trawl winch* is another labour-saving device. Imagine what it must have been like to manually pull up a huge net full of fish, with the water adding so much extra weight to the whole procedure. This winch can cope with huge weights and can haul the great net out of the water from 2,000 feet or more below the surface.

The *skipper's quarters* often include the mate's and the boatswain's quarters below deck. Woe betide anyone getting it wrong since the men who hold those positions jealously guard their privileges. Naturally these are small cabins but they remain the private domains of the senior crew.

The *fo'c'sle* is the crew's favourite area since this is their sleeping quarters and the only place where they can get away from the bad weather. Usually quite cramped when crew members rest, the place is almost always littered with boots and coats, ready for pulling them back on at a moment's notice. Privacy? What's that?

The *gallows* might sound like the place where the skipper deals out the ultimate punishment to wayward crew members but in fact it is the hanging device for trawls which allows them to hang over the side of the vessel.

The *deck working area* is one of the coldest places on the planet if the vessel is in the Arctic during the winter. It is of course the place where the fish are landed, gutted and washed and there is hardly room to swing a catfish when that is going on.

The *fish hold* is exactly what it sounds like. It is usually divided into compartments in which there are shelves of fish in blocks or laid out over slabs of ice. Around 175 tons of fish can be stored in the average trawler and a full fish hold makes a skipper and his crew very happy.

The *galley and messroom* is the second favourite area for the crew. This is where they eat and relax with a game of cards or a good book, or perhaps even listening to radio commentary of a Grimsby Town football match, if that can be described as relaxing. This is also the place where the gentle art of being nice to the cook is not only developed but put into serious practice.

If that is not enough to remember, take a look at the *wheelhouse* again. It is a complicated area all of its own but has to function efficiently or the vessel will go nowhere in particular and catch nothing at all.

The *wheel* is the focal point of course and today it is usually power-assisted like the steering wheel of a modern vehicle. There was a time when only manpower could move it and that sometimes took more than one pair of hands on a heavy, stormy sea.

The *wheel indicator* reveals the exact position of the rudder, yet another dial to watch.

The *ship's telegraph*'s handle is connected to another telegraph in the engine room and records the speed at which the vessel is travelling. You and I would probably call it a speedometer.

The *radar screen* can identity land from about 100 miles, a large vessel from 30 miles and another trawler from about 10 miles. It is, of course, one of today's on-board essentials and makes life a lot safer than it was yesterday.

The *echo sounder* is another fantastic invention at which fishermen of a century ago would have marvelled. Signals are bounced off the sea-bed, enabling contours to be traced. Just as importantly to fishing vessels, fish and plankton can also be identified. We have much to thank dolphins and whales for as they showed us what could be done.

The *searchlight switch* is another of those little gadgets that can be easily overlooked and yet is so important. Anyone who falls into the sea in the middle of the night will testify to the importance of knowing where the searchlight switch can be found.

The *air whistle* might not seem very important but elsewhere in this book we read how a skipper and his crew owe their very lives to a whistle so once again, it is not put in place for fun but as an essential.

The *electric siren* does a similar job to the whistle but can be used to warn both crew or nearby vessels of a problem. Best to know where the switch is, just in case.

The *Decca navigator* is a bit more complicated than the previous three items mentioned here. Three coloured clocks each receive different signals. The readings allow the trawler's position to be plotted extremely accurately on a chart and this is probably the most valuable of all the aids provided to skippers for a safe and successful voyage.

The *dummy clock* is not exactly what it sounds. It is not a clock that can be changed to suit the mood. It is in fact a recording clock, registering times of events and functions, especially hauling times. With so much paperwork to be filled in and legislation to be adhered to, gadgets like these are also essentials.

The *ship's log* is not something you throw on the fire in the boiler room (remember, a novice might believe anything…) but an essential which registers and records the distance travelled through the water and may be used in evidence – a bit like tachometers in trucks.

The *direction finder* is a brilliant instrument which plots the vessel's position by cross-referring signals transmitted by different stations ashore.

The *magnetic compass* is basically one of the oldest traditional pieces of equipment on board except that it has changed through the years. It is now a telescopic attachment to a compass set in a binnacle above the bridge. Magnetic compasses had to be taken care of. They were both checked and serviced regularly and a careful eye had to be kept on them to make sure that no metal, with the exception of brass, was placed anywhere near the compass as this could totally disrupt its accuracy. It is no accident or for ornamental reasons that metal fittings on board are mostly brass.

The *revolution counter* records the speed of the ship and is thus very useful if the skipper ever has to say: 'Really officer? I'm sure I wasn't doing more than 60.'

There are three other items the novice or apprentice needed – and still needs – to become familiar with as he (or she) learns the language of fishing:

The *voice pipe* might sound like something that Fishermen's Friend lozenges would sort out but in fact it is the old-fashioned means of communication from the bridge to other parts of the vessel. Usually one pipe went to the skipper's quarters and another to the engine room. Make a mistake when the captain is taking a rare rest at your peril.

The *Aldis lamp* is used to, well, let us describe it as a narrow beam of light. That gives a clue. Yes, it is a morse code signal light to be used if radio communication collapses.

The *wireless* has been a close friend of fishing folk for many years. When you are out there on the ocean and especially around the Dogger Bank or one of those other famous areas, you never want to miss the weather forecasts and, of course, the shipping forecasts. Your life might depend upon it so no bridge will be without its wireless.

So that's the equipment but there is something else the newcomer needs to know and those are the superstitions associated with the long traditions of the industry. Some of those seem to be defunct these days but might be worth noting if you are on your first trip and don't want to be thrown overboard!

Never empty the teapot. Perhaps that is outdated as most of us use tea bags these days but on a trawler in the freezing seas of Iceland and even further north, tea was vital and available virtually non-stop. If anyone emptied the teapot that was bad news and could have the crew grumbling in minutes. Better to keep it full and ready.

Certain words were considered unutterable while at sea. You avoided using the words 'clergy', 'church', 'knife', 'salt', 'pig', 'rat', 'rabbit' or 'egg'. That meant some improvisation of course but did not impair communication once you learned the alternative language.

Never wear green. That is quite common in various walks of life. In the theatre and circus, green is considered to be an unlucky colour, as indeed it is on board a trawler. Be careful when you choose your sweater.

Never look back or turn to face land once you have set sail. This was considered to be a bad omen that the trip could be unsuccessful, or worse, it might be the last time you see land – ever.

It was considered very unlucky to have a woman on board. That is not exclusive to fishing folk of course as many other ships, having nothing to do with fishing, have been unhappy about having a woman on board, even when picking up survivors. In modern shipping with huge tankers and freight ships, many skippers take their wives with them – but you don't hear much about trawlerwomen, do you?

It was also thought to be unlucky if a ship's name was changed or if the name ended with the letter 'e' or even included the letter 's'. By the law of averages there must have been a good percentage of ships lost that included those letters, but equally as many survived to a ripe old age before heading for the scrapyard.

Here's a good one – *tins should not be opened upside down* in case the vessel should overturn. That put a bit of extra pressure on the cook who had to check to make sure that the can of beans was the right way up before he attacked it.

It is said that *many fishermen and other sailors did not learn to swim* as this might indicate a lack of faith in their survival chances.

Tattoos were regarded as protection against evil spirits. Not sure how that worked exactly but many tattoos involved spiritual slogans. Many also considered that tattoos were a good idea for identification in the event of them drowning. How times change. Most tattoos now are either fashion statements or an indication of having survived a particularly drunken bout.

Crews on a fishing vessel – like many others – were not to eat on board while wearing a hat or sou'wester. The idea of having rainwater off your sou'wester dripping onto your bacon, eggs and beans makes it more commonsense than superstition.

Then of course we have one of the old favourites – *'touch wood'*. On a fishing vessel you wouldn't say that, as it could be deemed to be unlucky. Instead, to encourage good luck you would say 'touch iron'.

So there you have it – things not to do or say. You may believe in them or not. Personally, I take them with a pinch of salt... oops!

Chapter 10

Laugh in the Face of Adversity

I t is often said that laughter is the best medicine and that is probably true. Laughter has helped countless people through very severe situations or just generally a rough way of life. The fishing industry provides just such a life for many and they have surely learned the value of laughter.

Perhaps that is one of the reasons that during fishing's hey-day the pubs, restaurants and theatres of Lincolnshire's coast always knew when the fishing fleet was in. The saloons and bars were full and the drink flowed as if it was an alcoholic monsoon.

One of the busiest pubs in Grimsby was the Freemans Arms, which regularly found itself packed to the doors. How there was ever room for a piano is a mystery but there was; as well as pianists to back the regular sing-along. Somehow there was also space for a game of darts and bar billiards and there are no reports of anyone being hit by a stray dart although it must surely have happened.

The Freemans Arms was typical of the pubs in the area. Freeman Street itself was always packed when the fishing men were back on shore – some even took their wives out! There was always the sound of singing, piano at full pelt and laughter, although it must be said that there was also the sound of raised voices as a prelude to raised fists.

Fishing folk have always liked to let their hair down in many different ways. While some just ate, drank, sang and argued, others enjoyed the theatre, the picture house and sports events, of which the most popular was watching Grimsby Town, a football club with a more illustrious past than present.

The Freemans Arms has for very many years been one of the focal points for Grimsby fishing folk. Not only is it a favourite watering hole but the local centre for socialising, business transactions, buying and selling, arguments and friendship forging.

The Mariners, as they are affectionately known, began life as Grimsby Pelham in 1878 and have been taking fishing folk on an adventure of delight and despair ever since, a mirror image of life on the ocean wave. They have been in the top division of English football as well as the bottom, they have been to Wembley more than once, and had among their number such stars as the legendary Bill Shankly. Along with Hull City they were given special permission to play Football League matches on Christmas Day because of the schedules demanded by the fishing industry. The Mariners also made it a tradition to present visiting clubs with a box of fish to take home. This was always popular among those visiting clubs although one can only wonder about the condition of the fish after a long haul back to Torquay.

Further down the coast, Boston United have provided the football entertainment since 1933 and, like Grimsby have also had something of an up and down history which certainly matches the local fishing industry.

But football and other sports interests have always been in the reserves compared with the first team entertainment of the pub. 'Where you have fishing, no matter which part of the world, there has always been a drinking culture attached and Lincolnshire is no exception,' said former trawlerman John Vincent. 'The pub is where friendships and camaraderie are sealed or broken, where goods change hands, where future wives are often met, where recruitment takes place and games are played. The pub is the very hub of life and the nearer the docks the better.

'Most seamen would go home, take a few little gifts for the family and just be there for a while before heading for the pub, with or without his wife. Sadly some made for the pub as soon as they were paid and did not emerge until they were broke and totally drunk.

'Some would also head for the pub for a last drink before they embarked on another voyage. You could see them staggering towards the vessel and more people have fallen into the water after missing their footing through drink than anything else. I hope that doesn't paint too black a picture because it was not the fault of the pub, which actually provided a home from home for many excellent men.'

Because of the hazardous life they led and still lead, fishing folk like to laugh and that is why comedians have always been particularly popular in local theatres, clubs and even pubs, where most comics will tell you that they are in competition with the voices of the audience.

Freddie Frinton, an internationally acclaimed comedy star of both pre-war and post-war periods, was not only born in Grimsby but in the fishing industry. His father was a trawlerman and it was quite clear that young Freddie Hargate – his real name – was destined to follow him into the industry. Freddie was not so keen on going to sea though and at the age of 14 he left school and began working as a fish curer. Even at that age he could not resist making his workmates laugh. His sense of timing was not so good in those days though. On one occasion he stopped work to entertain the others just as the boss walked in and brought down the curtain on his job.

At the suggestion of another local entertainer, Mark Hardy, Freddie began appearing as a comic in pubs in the area. He didn't earn very much but he gained a lot in terms of the material he would put to good use as his act developed. For anyone who has never heard of Freddie Frinton, he mastered the art of playing a comic drunk to absolute perfection.

At last Freddie became a real entertainer when producer Jimmy Slater paid him £3 per week to appear in a variety show on Cleethorpes Pier. Agents and other producers saw him and from that springboard in the resort Freddie was launched into London and on major theatre tours. It was all building quite nicely until the Second World War broke out. Freddie joined the Royal Artillery but was soon signed up as one of the Stars In Battledress, a group of entertainers who kept up morale by taking part in shows for members of the forces. He entertained thousands of troops in various parts of the world, as well as at home and, of course, that added to his experience and material.

At the end of the war he was instantly engaged to appear in a major pantomime in London and once again the agents and bookers were queuing at his door. His greatest achievement was probably co-starring with Thora Hird in a TV comedy series called *Meet the Wife*, which attracted around fifteen million viewers to each episode.

Freddie died in 1968 but he never forgot his roots in the Lincolnshire fishing industry. He often spent time in his home town and once said: 'I had the best education in the world, learning how to make people in the fishing industry laugh. It is a tough business with a hard way of life. There are so many opportunities for sadness that if you can get people laughing when they are under that sort of pressure then you know you can do it anywhere.'

Just to keep the record straight, Freddie Frinton was not a real drunk. He would drink in extreme moderation and learned his skill from observing those around him. He had plenty of opportunities, of course.

At the various theatres and cinemas that have abounded in the fishing towns of Lincolnshire, such other comics as the county's own Arthur Lucan (perhaps best known as Old Mother Riley) Tommy Trinder, Jimmy Jewel and Ben Warriss, Morecambe and Wise, Norman Collier, Norman Wisdom and even the legendary Laurel and Hardy have all had them rolling in the aisles. Ken Dodd is still a regular visitor to the Lincolnshire coast.

'I love coming to Lincolnshire and especially the coast,' said Doddy. 'It is not just the holidaymakers but the local people and you can always tell if they are in the fishing industry – they have a whole row to themselves. I was once asked to go into fishing, I think they thought I could frighten off the sharks.

'All joking aside for a moment, just a moment, I have a great deal of respect for those who bring back the fish, it must be one of the hardest jobs around, even harder than playing first house at Glasgow Empire all those years ago. Fishing people know how to have fun though. They love to laugh and it shows. They don't laugh behind their hands, they go for it full throttle and have fun. I really like that.

'We all owe them a huge thank you for the fish they have brought to our local chippie. By the way, don't tell them in Blackpool I said this, but Lincolnshire fish and chips is probably the best there is, even better than Scarborough and that's saying something. By the way, did you hear about the fish and chip shop owner who locked himself out? He had to batter the door down!

'Keep on trawling lads, you're doing a fantastic job!'

A trawlerman who made the transition into entertainment was Bunny Newton, who skippered vessels through the icy waters of the Arctic Circle and took on the gunboats of Iceland during those famous Cod Wars. All the time he nursed a hunger for entertainment and eventually he was able to open Bunny's Place, a 1,000-seater theatre club which attracted stars from all over the world. The first artiste to appear there in May 1975 was comedian Frankie Howerd, once again proving that fishing folk love to laugh. The list that followed in the years to come was quite a who's who of show business from Charles Aznavour to Roger Whitaker, with Eartha Kitt, Roy Orbison, Frankie Vaughan, the Shadows and just about every other famous name of the time included.

Bunny's Place eventually became a victim of the economy and when its captain, Bunny Newton, died, that was the end of an era. It is gone but not forgotten, just like Bunny, the man who had a dream at sea and made it come true on land, providing entertainment for his former shipmates.

The cinema made a big impact in the fishing towns as it did everywhere during the first half of the 20th century, but perhaps it was the dance halls which remained consistently popular and provided that first meeting which led to so many marriages. One of the most popular in Grimsby was the Gaiety which was regularly packed as fishing folk let their hair down. In Boston, the Gliderdrome was the most popular venue and many recall romances that began with a waltz or a jive.

As we said at the start, the bars were more than popular and there were so many to choose from. One of the most celebrated among the young was Taddies on the Cleethorpes promenade. It was often intended to be the meeting place for a night out with young trawlermen and their girlfriends heading there first before perhaps going dancing. Everyone knew where it was and it became a local landmark. The evening was regularly rearranged too, since people liked Taddies so much they forgot the rest of their plans and stayed there for the entire evening. It was just that kind of a place.

Fun fairs, circuses, talent shows, galas and all kind of other entertainments have been enthusiastically supported throughout the centuries right down to this day as the fishing folk put away their worries and enjoy themselves by laughing in the face of adversity.

Chapter 11

The Future

eal fishing folk say they would not change their lives for all the tea in China even though the money could be better, the hours are long and hard and socially it is far from perfect. The job is clearly life-threatening yet, for all their talk, hardly any of them would really want to change it. But the question remains – does the fishing industry and its unique community still have a future in Lincolnshire?

It is obvious that the fishing industry in general has drifted with the tide. Sometimes the financial water has been quite deep and comfortable for the thousands of people involved. Other times, the tide seems to become low before our very eyes and boats and people are the victims. Let's face it, fishing has known better days. Grimsby was indeed the biggest fishing port in the world at one time and elsewhere along the Lincolnshire coast there was a knock-on effect of prosperity. The tide went out though and the industry was crippled.

Why did it all go wrong? There have been times when the demand for fish waned and the economy made it a non-viable pursuit. The fish stocks are, understandably not what they were. You cannot indiscriminately take without giving something back, as the source will eventually be so depleted as to dry up. Those lessons have hopefully been learned and we have entered a new age of fishing which might not recapture the past glories but will at least safeguard the industry's future.

There is certainly an air of optimism in Lincolnshire fishing these days. Grimsby is now as well known for being a fish trading centre as for being the home of fishing. The relationship with Iceland is much better again these days and fish from the former aggressors is now often landed at Grimsby as it was years ago when the town was in its hey-day.

Jon Bjarnason, Icelandic Minister for Fisheries and Agriculture, said that he was very impressed on his visit to Grimsby in June 2009: 'I knew all about the heritage of Grimsby before I visited and I was not at all disappointed. There has clearly been investment of both money and enthusiasm and that can only be good for the future. On my visit it was busy too and that is a good sign. Grimsby has always been about fish and it is great to see that there is still a strong fishing community here. I hope that the ties between us grow stronger and stronger.'

Another sign of optimism is the number of Lincolnshire companies engaged either directly or indirectly in the fishing industry. Many of them are fairly new businesses and that has to show great confidence in the future.

Grimsby and Lincolnshire in general are always well represented at international food and trade fairs. Professor Mike Dillon sits on the boards of several allied organisations, as well as being president of the International Association of Fish Inspectors. He often represents the area at trade shows and reports a great interest in doing business with Grimsby. 'I attend many of these events and I really want to fly the flag for Grimsby,' he said. 'These shows do provide some great opportunities and I have to say that Grimsby has a very good reputation around the world. There are many companies and countries who want to do business with us.'

Others echo that view and there is a great deal of hard work going on behind the scenes to ensure a bright future for the industry in Lincolnshire. One of those hard-working organisations constantly keeping its members to the fore of the fishing world is the Grimsby Fish Merchants Association. Let's face it, without the merchants there is no industry so the work of this particular association is vital.

Formed in 1911, the GFMA has seen many developments, boom years and years of strife of one sort or another. There are currently more than 100 members of the Association, which is the only full-time such organisation in the country. The same offices also run the Federation of British Port Wholesale Fish Merchants Association, a very pro-active lobby group.

Although the GFMA is a fairly low-profile organisation it has earned a lot of respect for its hard work in protecting and promoting the fishing industry. One of its great contributions to the local industry is its Fish Settlement scheme which enables agents, vessel owners, merchants and suppliers to be paid within ten days. That involves transactions exceeding £1 million every week and has helped many local businesses to swim rather than sink.

Chief executive Steve Norton said: 'Like any other business it can be a struggle sometimes to fit in with the economy, consider carefully any government proposals and take whatever action is deemed necessary as well as supporting individual businesses of various sizes and activities. We are optimistic about the future though. We have confidence that every problem can be overcome by communication and common sense. Things don't stay the same, they change and you just have to change with them.'

Another organisation, the Grimsby Fishing Vessel Owners Association, has been around for half a century in its current guise but actually began life back in 1878 as the Great Grimsby Smack

Owners' Association. These days the association includes fish-selling agents and also provides the industry with a voice, so important in today's maze of legislation.

Together these organisations are all optimistic about the future of Lincolnshire's fishing industry as indeed is the National Fishing Heritage Centre's resident expert John Vincent.

'The oceans are huge and conservation plans have meant an increase in some fish stocks so I think we can be optimistic about the future,' he said. 'That doesn't mean that it will ever go back to the golden years with hundreds of trawlers and thousands of men going to sea. We will never see that again because it was a different world at a different time.

'The important thing is that the demand for fish is still there and does not decline. The danger is that we import too much and do not take care of the British fishing industry. There are still thousands of people involved in fish processing here in Lincolnshire and that is a good thing. Not so good is the amount of fish brought here by means other than being landed from trawlers.

'All the restrictions and legislation that swamp fishing do not make it easy for anyone with an entrepreneurial spirit. By the time you have been bogged down with quotas and heath and safety, it is a miracle that anyone actually sets out to fish.

'Having said that, the fishing industry has proven its ability to keep going by adapting and changing its course when needed. We don't have sailing boats and hand-hauled nets anymore. You have to move on to survive and the Lincolnshire fishing industry is nothing if it is not a survivor.'

Chapter 12

The National Fishing Heritage Centre

As an island race, the British have an affinity with water and fish that goes way beyond the local chip shop. Fishing is part of Lincolnshire's history and, even more importantly, a part of our national heritage. When the idea of a National Fishing Heritage Centre was first mooted, therefore, there could only be one place for it to be built and that was as near as possible to Grimsby Fish Docks. Even so, nobody, however optimistic and enthusiastic, could have envisaged just how successful this project was going to be.

After careful design and creation and some very special marketing and publicity treatment, the Centre finally opened its doors in 1991. It has since won many awards and compliments both from visitors who have never set foot on a trawler and from those experienced

The National Fishing Heritage Centre in Grimsby. Walk through these doors and you will find yourself stepping back in time to a fascinating journey through the highs and lows, toil and leisure of the entire industry.

fishing folk who really know whether or not it is representative of the industry.

The Heritage Centre covers all aspects and eras of the fishing industry both in Lincolnshire and in Britain in general, but its particular theme centres on the boom times of the 1950s when Grimsby was indeed the busiest fishing port in the world. Perhaps this section from the NFHC's own brochure describes it best:

The National Fishing Heritage Centre recreates the industry in its heyday, capturing the atmosphere and the essence of the period – from Bill Haley and the Comets to Brylcream and Cod Liver Oil.

You experience this twentieth century saga. Signing on as a crew member and travelling on the journey of a lifetime – from the back streets of Grimsby to the Arctic fishing grounds. You feel the pitch and roll of the ship, the urgency and excitement of the catch, the raw, icy blast of the wind, the cramped living conditions, the heat of the engine room, the hubbub of the radio room and authority of the bridge.

The sights, the sounds, the drama – the experience will leave you with a new respect for the men who for centuries have pitted their strength against the elements to bring home the catch.

A young visitor to the National Fishing Heritage Centre finds out first-hand what it was like on the trawlers in days of undulating waves and icebergs.

I have been there and it is quite an experience, and it certainly does bring home much more of what fishing is about and has been about for all these years. The visitor can sense the danger without experiencing it. You can sense the seasickness without actually… well, er, you can experience the seasickness. Better take a coat when you walk through the ice room, it's freezing. Mind you, you definitely won't need a coat in the boiler room when you feel the contrasting heat of the place.

That's not all, since the quayside shop is a nostalgia trip, reminding us of the goods and prices on offer when fishing was in its heyday.

If anything, that brochure extract actually underestimates the value of the National Fishing Heritage Centre. The amazing reconstructions of the back streets of Grimsby, the tension in the household waiting for news of a missing trawler and the smiles on the faces of the fishing folk relaxing in the recreated Freemans Arms pub give a real feel of life amid the fishing community.

For me, the recreation of the galley, with the cook doing his best to keep the pots boiling and the bread toasting while the vessel is being tossed around on a heavy sea, is well worth the visit on its own.

Moored alongside the NFHC but a part of its attraction is the *Ross Tiger*, of which we spoke some pages ago and definitely not to be missed if you want to get an even more authentic feel of fishing life.

John Vincent is the chief tour guide for the whole Centre: 'We have tried to give people more than just knowledge, we try to give them the experience,' he said. 'I thoroughly enjoy taking the groups around the Centre and onto the *Tiger* whether those groups are schoolchildren or grown-ups, many of whom might be former trawlermen themselves. Every time I take a tour I step back in time to a life I have both led and loved. There is nothing quite like it and I am delighted that so many people are interested.

'There are a number of souvenirs of fishing's past here, genuine examples of how it all worked in days gone by and where actual items could not be found, replicas have been used. The street scenes, the parlours, the vessel quarters, the bridge and all the other displays are as real as can be without being out there and a part of the sea fishing life.

Thousands of visitors do flock to the National Fishing Heritage Centre throughout the year and many letters of thanks and compliments are received from those visitors. One was from a little girl who simply said: 'I thought it was going to be a museum of glass cases but I was wrong. It is so real, it is like being on a real boat.'

Inspiration

The fishing industry has been inspirational to many during its history. Folk songs are still sung in clubs and pubs about fishing, many of them decades, if not centuries old and still popular. Books and poems have been written, films produced and, of course countless photographs have been taken. There have also been many paintings created and one of the most celebrated artists in Lincolnshire is Steve Farrow of Cleethorpes, who was born in 1963 to a family with a strong seafaring background.

'That inspired my interest in the sea and ships and especially fishing,' Steve explained. 'As a youngster during school holidays I liked nothing better than to sail on trawlers as a kind of pleasure trip whenever the opportunity arose.'

Steve went on to the nautical school in Grimsby and from there to the Merchant Navy as a cadet, deck apprentice. Then he spent 17 years with Associated British Ports, much of that time on the Humber where he continued to find himself drawn to the trawlers making their way to and from the North Sea and Arctic fishing grounds.

'I started taking photographs and sketching various vessels and the more I did the more I wanted to do. I started painting them in oils but then changed to watercolour because it seemed to suit my style so much better.'

When trawler owners and skippers saw some of Steve's work they began to commission paintings of their own vessels. 'I have been painting them ever since,' he said. 'These days it is mostly from old photographs because those trawlers are just not around anymore but I find even the photographs are just totally inspiring. There is something about ships and especially something about fishing vessels which fires the imagination and the inspiration to paint them.'

If you would like to view Steve's work, take a look at the website www.trawlerart.com.

Lincolnshire-born fisherman writer and video producer Mark Stopper understandably laments the obvious decline of fishing but still finds himself inspired by it.

'There is no doubt that the industry has been run down,' he said. 'It all changed after the Cod War. The exclusion zone put around Iceland really messed it all up. The fish prefer coastal waters for feeding so not being able to go within 200 miles of the Icelandic coast meant severe cutbacks in the amount of fish being brought home.

'The other side of the coin is that the fish in that area are plentiful and now there is beginning to be just a little relaxation of the restrictions. At the same time I believe there is a good future in The Wash. There are probably too many boats going out to The Wash at the moment, for shellfish. They are chasing too few species but with proper management there is every chance that the industry will thrive there.

'As for me, I enjoy still being on the fringe of it all but even though I am now around 50 and still young enough to go deep sea fishing, I have a dream that I and others like me will one day have the chance to return full-time once again to the unique life of the fishing boats.'

It is that kind of inspiration and desire that drives so many people on to remain close to the hardest industry in the world. Fishing folk are eternally optimistic, they have to be. If they were not, they simply couldn't do it.

On Reflection ... and Acknowledgements

Life seems to get faster and faster. Sadly, food has fallen into the same speed trap and we are well and truly hooked on fast food and if it can be delivered to our door so much the better. But there is one take-away that still shines above all others – good old fish and chips. Where would we be without that golden batter surrounding a piece of nutritional cod or haddock, accompanied by a battalion of finely cooked chips made from those well-turned-out British potatoes? Let us, then, celebrate the traditional fish and chips.

Inside the chip shop the atmosphere was almost party-like. The busy staff kept up a constant repartee of football banalities interspersed with comments on the weather, the Royal family, holidays at Butlins, Mrs Jones' youngest taking her first steps and the sadness of old Bill, a revered war veteran, having passed away in the previous night.

The chip shop was not just the place for fish and chips, pickled onions and salt and vinegar. It was the hub of local news and a haven for the hungry and the poorly paid who could get a meal for a few pence. It was a crowded world of anticipation, an eagerness to clutch the newspaper parcel in which your battered treasure had been wrapped. Perhaps you would be eating them at home with a glass of lemonade. Perhaps, especially on holiday, you would have them open and eat them as you strolled, rolling a very hot chip from one side of your mouth to the other until you dared to bite and swallow.

Yesterday chips were greasy, dripping with hot animal fat. Today they are mostly cooked in vegetable oil. Yesterday you might have the extra treat of a pickled onion or a gherkin – a 'wally', as they were sometimes called. Today mushy peas or curry sauce are the extras. Yesterday you might find them wrapped in last Saturday's evening paper – the pink sports edition – and as you walked you could remind yourself of the football results from that weekend. Today, the wrapping paper is invariably white and possibly surrounding a polystyrene tray.

But the fish and chip shop still provides something quite unique, a friendliness in which even strangers can take part. Yet it is under pressure. There are now so many variations of take-away and such a concerted advertising campaign to promote particular fast food franchises to young people that the fish and chip shop, which largely stands as an individual and alone in the fight for customers, is an endangered species. Add to their woes the increased price of fish and other running costs and it does not take long to see why the fish and chip shop is wilting.

Let us never forget that we are an island race, surrounded by the ocean and capable of growing the best potatoes in the world. Let us make sure that we never neglect the industry that has risked so much and sometimes lost lives just to provide for our table. Yes, let's hear it for the folk past and present who are the very life of that fishing industry. To each and every one of them, from skipper to lumper, and from owner to apprentice, and their families – thank you.

and also … Thank You

What I knew about the Lincolnshire fishing industry before writing this you could have put on the back of a postcard. That doesn't mean that I had no interest, far from it. I have always had great admiration for the men and women who work hard and, in many cases, risk their lives for the sake of bringing home food for our tables.

The point is that I needed help in completing this book and therefore I should like to thank John Vincent, the National Fishing Heritage Centre, Steve Farrow, Mark Stopper, the *Grimsby Telegraph*, visitlincolnshire.com and the local authorities of Grimsby and Boston. It might not have happened without you.

Index